J7
10

LIFE OF GOLDSMITH.

LIFE

OF

OLIVER GOLDSMITH.

BY

AUSTIN DOBSON

KENNIKAT PRESS
Port Washington, N. Y./London

LIFE OF OLIVER GOLDSMITH

First published in 1888
Reissued in 1972 by Kennikat Press
Library of Congress Catalog Card No: 79-160753
ISBN 0-8046-1570-5

Manufactured by Taylor Publishing Company   Dallas, Texas

CONTENTS.

CHAPTER I.

CHAPTER II.

CHAPTER VIII.

CHAPTER IX.

CHAPTER X.

LIFE OF GOLDSMITH.

CHAPTER I.

IF the researches of the first biographers of Oliver Goldsmith are to be relied upon, the Goldsmith family was of English origin, the Irish branch having migrated from this country to Ireland somewhere about the sixteenth century. One of the earliest members traced by Prior was a certain John Goldsmyth, who, in 1541, held the office of searcher in the port of Galway, and was shortly afterwards promoted by Henry VIII. to be Clerk of the Council. A descendant of this John, according to tradition, married one Juan Romeiro, a Spanish gentleman, who, having travelled in Ireland, finally took up his abode there. His children, retaining the name and the Protestant faith of their mother, settled in Roscommon, Longford, and Westmeath, where of old many traces of them existed which have now disappeared. Some became clergymen, and, during the rebellion of 1641, did not escape the animosity attaching to their cloth. Nor was this their solitary distinction. The maiden name of James Wolfe's mother was Goldsmith, and the Goldsmiths consequently claimed kinship with the conqueror of Quebec. Another and more shadowy connection was supposed to exist with Oliver Cromwell, from whom the poet was wont to declare that his own Christian name was derived. But as his maternal grandfather was called Oliver Jones, it is probable that no great importance need be attached to this assertion. It is more to the point to note that the whole of the Irish Goldsmiths seem to have been distinguished by common characteristics. Even as, in the later " Vicar of Wakefield," the " Blenkinsops could never look straight before them, nor the Hugginses blow out a candle," so the actual ancestors of the author of that immortal book have a marked mental likeness. They may, indeed, be described in almost the exact words applied to the Primrose family. They were " all equally generous, credulous, simple," and improvident.

But the further history of the first Goldsmiths may be neglected in favour of that particular member of the race in whom, for the moment, this biography is chiefly interested—the Rev. Charles Goldsmith of Pallas, Oliver Goldsmith's father. Charles Goldsmith was the second son of Robert Goldsmith of Ballyoughter, by his wife Catherine, daughter of Thomas Crofton, D.D., sometime dean of Elphin. In 1707, he went to Trinity College, Dublin, as a pensioner, passing through it with credit. Among his university associates, it was said by his son, was Parnell the poet, and he is also believed to have been acquainted with Swift's friend—" the punster, quibbler, fiddler and wit," Thomas Sheridan, grandfather of the author of the " School for Scandal." In May, 1718, Charles Goldsmith married Ann, daughter of the Rev. Oliver Jones, master of the diocesan school at Elphin,

where he himself had been educated.   Having taken this
step without means, and his father-in-law being also a
poor man, his prospects were of the vaguest.   But his
wife's uncle, the Rev. Mr. Green of Kilkenny West,
offered the young couple an asylum at Pallas or Pallasmore
in Longford, not very far from the town of Ballymahon.
It was a tumbledown, fairy-haunted farmhouse overlooking
the pleasant river Inny, which runs through Ballymahon
to Lough Ree; and here, while he divided his time
between farming a few fields and assisting Mr. Green in
his clerical duties, five children were born to Charles
Goldsmith—three girls, Margaret, Catherine, and Jane;
and two boys, Henry and Oliver.   The last named, who
saw the light on November 10, 1728, is the subject of
these pages.

When Oliver Goldsmith was born, his father's annual
income as a curate and farmer, even when swelled by the
contributions of friends, amounted to no more than forty
pounds.   But two years later Mr. Green died, and
Charles Goldsmith succeeded to the vacant Rectory of
Kilkenny West, transferring his residence to Lissoy, a
little village on the right of the road from Ballymahon to
Athlone.   His house, which was connected with the
highway by a long avenue of ash-trees, had an orchard
and a pleasant garden at the back.   The new living was
worth nearly two hundred a year; and here Charles Goldsmith continued to maintain that kindly hospitable household, which his son sketched later in the narrative of the
"Man in Black."   "His education was above his fortune,
and his generosity greater than his education.   Poor as he
was, he had his flatterers still poorer than himself; for

every dinner he gave them, they returned him an equivalent in praise. . . . He told the story of the ivy-tree,
and that was laughed at ; he repeated the jest of the two
scholars and one pair of breeches, and the company
laughed at that ; but the story of Taffy in the sedan chair
was sure to set the table in a roar." Neither his practice
nor his precepts were those which make rich men.
Learning, he held, was better than silver or gold, and
benevolence than either. In this way he brought up his
children to be " mere machines of pity," and " perfectly
instructed them in the art of giving away thousands before
they were taught the more necessary qualifications of
getting a farthing."

In the meantime little Oliver was transferred to the
care of Elizabeth Delap, a relative and dependant, who
taught him his letters. Years afterwards, when she was
an old woman of ninety, she described this as no easy
task. Her pupil, she affirmed, was exceedingly dull
and stupid, although she admitted that he was easily
managed. From this unflattering instructress he passed
to the far more congenial tuition of the village schoolmaster, Thomas Byrne. Byrne was a character in his
way, some of whose traits reappear in the pedagogue of
" The Deserted Village." He had been a soldier in
Queen Anne's wars in Spain, and had led a wandering
adventurous life, of which he was always willing to talk.
He was besides something of a bookman, dabbled in
rhyme, and was even capable of extemporizing a respect-
able Irish version of Virgil's eclogues. Furthermore, in
addition to being an adept in all the fairy lore of Ireland,
he was deeply read in the records of its pirates, robbers, and

smugglers. One can imagine little Oliver hanging upon the lips of this entrancing teacher, when he discoursed, not only of "the exploits of Peterborough and Stanhope, the surprise of Monjuich, and the glorious disaster of Brihuega," but also of ghosts and banshees, and of "the great Rapparee chiefs, Baldearg O'Donnell and galloping Hogan." No wonder the boy's friends traced to these distracting narratives his aimless, vagrant future. He, too, began to scribble doggerel, to devour the chap-book histories of "Fair Rosamond" and the "Seven Champions," or to study with avidity the less edifying chronicles of "Moll Flanders" and "Jack the Bachelor."

There were, moreover, other influences at this time to stir his childish imagination, which could scarcely have found him the "impenetrably stupid" pupil of his first mistress. There were the songs of the blind harper, O'Carolan, to awaken in him a love of music which he never lost, and there was Peggy Golden, his father's dairy-maid, to charm his ears with "Johnny Armstrong's Last Good Night," or "The Cruelty of Barbara Allen." But an untoward circumstance served to interrupt, if not to end, these "violent delights." So severely was he attacked by confluent small-pox that he nearly lost his life, and ever afterwards bore the traces of that disorder deeply scored upon his features. Indeed, it may be said to have also left its mark upon his character. Always "subject to particular humours," alternating often between extreme reserve and boisterous animal spirits, his natural tendencies were not improved by his changed appearance. One of the earliest anecdotes recorded of him turns upon this misfortune. "Why,

Noll!" said an inconsiderate male relative, not particularly distinguished for his wisdom or integrity, "you are
become a fright! When do you mean to get handsome
again?" The boy moved uneasily to the window without replying, and the question was sneeringly repeated.
"I mean to get better, sir, when you do," he answered
at last. Upon another occasion, when there was a
party at his uncle's house, little Oliver capered forth,
in the pause between two country dances, and indulged
the company with a hornpipe. His seamed face and
his ungainly figure — for he was short and thick of
stature—excited considerable amusement, and the fiddler,
a youth named Cumming, called out "Æsop." But to
the surprise of the guests, the dancer promptly retorted—

> " Heralds ! proclaim aloud ! all saying,
>   See *Æsop* dancing, and his *Monkey* playing "—

a couplet which, even if it were based upon a recollection,
as is most probable, at all events served its purpose by
turning the laugh against the musician.

When these events took place he had already, for
some obscure reason, been transferred from Byrne's care
to the school at Elphin, of which his grandfather had
once been master ; and he was living with his father's
brother, John Goldsmith of Ballyoughter. The afore-
mentioned instances of his quickness, no doubt carefully
preserved and repeated by admiring relatives, were held
to be significant of latent parts ; and it was decided that,
notwithstanding the expenses of his elder brother Henry's
education, which were draining his father's scanty means,

he should have all attainable advantages. From Elphin, relatives apparently aiding, he was sent to Athlone to a school kept by a Mr. Campbell. It does not appear that he presented himself to his schoolfellows in the same light as to those of his family who saw him at his best. Dr. Annesley Strean, who, in later days, became curate of Kilkenny West, and conversed with many of Goldsmith's contemporaries, found him to have been regarded by them "as a stupid, heavy blockhead, little better than a fool, whom every one made fun of. But his corporal powers differed widely from this apparent state of his mind, for he was remarkably active and athletic; of which he gave proofs in all exercises among his playmates, and eminently in ball-playing, which he was very fond of, and practised whenever he could."

After he had been two years at Athlone, Mr. Campbell gave up the school from ill-health, and Oliver passed to the care of the Rev. Patrick Hughes of Edgeworthstown, a friend of his father. His happiest schooldays must have been with this master. Mr. Hughes understood him. He penetrated his superficial obtuseness, recognized his morbidly sensitive nature, and managed at any rate to think better of him than his playmates, many of whom only succeeded in growing up to be blockheads. At Edgeworthstown there were traditions of his studies, of his love for Ovid and Horace, of his hatred for Cicero and his delight in Livy and Tacitus, of his prowess in boyish sports and the occasional robbing of orchards. But the best anecdote of this time is one which belongs to the close of his last holidays, when he was between fourteen and fifteen years of age. Having set off for school on a borrowed hack, and equipped with boundless riches in the shape of a guinea given him by a friend, he amused himself by viewing the neighbouring country seats on the road, intending ultimately to put up like a gentleman at an inn. Night fell, and he found himself at Ardagh, half way on his journey. Casting about for information as to " the best house," that is to say, the best inn in the neighbourhood, he unluckily lit upon one Cornelius Kelly, who had been fencing-master to the Marquis of Granby, but, what is more to the purpose, was a confirmed wag and practical joker. Amused with Oliver's schoolboy swagger, he gravely directed him to the mansion of the local magnate, Squire Featherston. To Squire Featherston's the lad accordingly repaired, and called lustily for some one to take his horse. Being ushered into the presence of the supposed landlord and his family, he ordered a good supper, invited the rest to share it, treated them to a bottle or two of wine, and finally retired to rest, leaving careful injunctions that a hot cake should be prepared for his breakfast on the morrow. His host, who was a humourist, and moreover knew something of his visitor's father, never undeceived him; and it was not until he quitted the supposed inn next day that he learned, to his confusion, that he had been entertained at a private house. Thus early in Oliver Goldsmith's career was rehearsed the first sketch of the successful comedy of " She Stoops to Conquer."

But the time was approaching when he was to enter upon the college life to which all his education had been tending. He had hoped to go to Trinity College as a

pensioner, like his brother Henry, who a year earlier had
triumphantly obtained a scholarship. This, however,
was not to be. Henry Goldsmith had been engaged as
tutor to the son of a gentleman named Hodson, residing
near Athlone, and out of this connection had resulted a
secret marriage between his pupil and his sister Catharine.
From a worldly point of view the match was an excellent
one, as the Hodsons were wealthy and well-to-do; but
the reproaches of the young man's father stung Charles
Goldsmith into taking a step which seriously crippled his
resources. He entered into an engagement to pay a
marriage portion of £400 with his daughter, and to this
end taxed his farm and tithes until it should be defrayed.
There was more of wounded pride than of strict justice
in this procedure, which must have kept his family pinched
until his death. The immediate result of it was a change
in the prospects of his second son. It was no longer
possible to send him to college as a pensioner; he
must go in a more economical way as a "sizar" or poor
scholar. At that time, as now, the sizars of Trinity
College were educated without charge; they had free
lodgings in the college garrets, and they were permitted
to "batten on cold bits" from the commons' table. But
in return for these privileges, they wore a distinctive
costume, and were required to perform certain menial
offices, now abolished. Young Oliver, endowed by
nature with "an exquisite sensibility of contempt"—
to use his later words—fought hard against this humiliating entry into academic life. For a long time he resisted
his fate; but finally, owing to the influence of a friendly
uncle, the Rev, Mr. Contarine, who had already assisted

in educating him, he yielded, and was admitted to Trinity College, Dublin, as a poor scholar, on the 11th of June, 1744, being then fifteen. In the lives of Forster and Prior, the year of admission is given as 1745 ; but this has been shown by Dr. J. F. Waller to be an error. Another Edgeworthstown pupil of the name of Beatty came with him; and the pair took up their abode in the garrets of what was then No. 35 in a range of buildings which has long since disappeared, but at that time formed the eastern side of Parliament Square.

If the circumstances of Goldsmith's initiation into college life were scarcely favourable to his idiosyncrasy, he was still more unfortunate in the tutor with whom he was placed. The Rev. Theaker Wilder, to whose care he fell, although a man of considerable ability, was apparently the last person in the world by whom his pupil's peculiarities could be indulgently or even temperately regarded. Wilder was a man of vindictive character, morose and, at times, almost ferocious in his demeanour. Once,—so the story goes,—with a sudden bound upon a passing hackney-coach, he felled to the ground its luckless driver, who had accidentally touched his face with his whip. Under such a master Goldsmith could but fare ill. His ungainly appearance, his awkwardness, and a certain mental unreadiness, which he never afterwards lost, except when he had pen in hand, left him wholly at the mercy of his persecutor, who saw in him nothing but the evidence of a dense and stubborn disposition. To make matters worse, Wilder delighted in mathematics, and Goldsmith detested them as much as Gray did. "This,"

he said later, in a passage which had more of bitter recollection than absolute accuracy—"seems a science, to
which the meanest intellects are equal. I forget who it is
that says 'All men might understand mathematics, if they
would.'" The "dreary subtleties" of "Dutch Burgers-
dyck" and Polish Smeglesius, the luminaries who then
presided over the study of logic, equally repelled him, as
they had repelled his predecessor, Swift. Everything was
thus against his advancement to honours, and the measure
of his disqualification was filled up by a certain idle
habit of "perpetually lounging about the college-gate,"
(of which, by the way, Johnson was also accused at
Oxford,) and by a boyish love of pleasure and
amusement. He sang with considerable taste: he played
passably upon the German flute. Both of these accom-
plishments made him popular with many of his fellows,
but they were not those from whose ranks the distinguished members of an university are usually recruited.

With these characteristics, that he should be associated
with the scandals rather than with the successes of an
academic career is perhaps to be anticipated. Accordingly, in May, 1747, we find him involved in a college
riot. A report had been circulated that a scholar had
been arrested in Fleet Street (Dublin). This was an
indignity to which no gownsman could possibly submit.
Led by a wild fellow called "Gallows" Walsh, who,
among the students, exercised the enviable and self-
conferred office of "Controller-General of tumults in
ordinary," they carried the bailiff's den by storm, stripped
the unfortunate wretch who was the chief offender, and
ducked him soundly in the college cistern. Intoxicated

by this triumph and reinforced by the town mob, they then proceeded to attack the tumble-down old prison known as the "Black Dog," with a view to a general gaol delivery. But the constable of that fortress, being a resolute man, well provided with firearms, made a gallant defence, the result being that two of the towns-men were killed and others wounded. Four of the ringleaders in this disastrous affair were expelled. Oliver Goldsmith was not among these; but having "aided and abetted," he was, with three others, publicly admonished, "*quod seditioni favisset et tumultuantibus opem tulisset.*"

From the stigma of this censure, he recovered shortly afterwards by a small success. He tried for a scholar-ship and failed; but he gained an exhibition amounting to some thirty shillings. Unhappily this only led to a fresh mishap. His elation prompted him to celebrate his good fortune by an entertainment at his rooms, which, to add to its enormity, included persons of both sexes. No sooner was the unwonted sound of a fiddle heard in the heights of No. 35, than the exasperated Wilder burst upon the assembly, dispersing the terrified guests, and, after a torrent of abuse, knocked down the hapless host. The disgrace was overwhelming. Hastily gathering his books together, the poor lad sold them for what they would fetch, and fairly ran away, vaguely bound for America. He loitered, however, in Dublin until his means were reduced to a shilling, and then set out for Cork. After reaching perilously close to starva-tion—for he afterwards told Reynolds that a handful of grey peas, given to him at this time by a good-natured girl at a wake, was the most comfortable repast he had ever made—he recovered his senses, and turned his steps homewards. His brother Henry (his father, the Rev. Charles Goldsmith, having died some three months earlier) came halfway to meet and receive him. Ultimately a kind of reconciliation was patched up with his tutor, and he was restored to the arms of his *Alma Mater*.

Henceforth his university life was less eventful. Wilder still, after his fashion, pursued his pupil with taunts and irony. But, beyond frequent "turnings - down," the college records contain no further evidence of unusual irregularity. His pecuniary supplies, always doubtful, had become more uncertain since his father's death, and now consisted chiefly of intermittent contributions from kind-hearted Uncle Contarine, and other friends. Often he must have been wholly dependent upon petty loans from his schoolmate Beatty, from his cousin Robert Bryanton, from his relative Edward Mills of Roscommon, — all of whom were his contemporaries at Trinity. Sometimes he was reduced to pawn his books —"*mutare quadrata rotundis*, like the silly fellow in Horace,"—as Wilder classically put it. Another method of making money, to which he occasionally resorted, was ballad-writing of a humble kind. There was a shop at the sign of the Rein-deer in Mountrath Court, where, at five shillings a head, he found a ready market for his productions, and it is related that he would steal out at nightfall to taste that supreme delight of the not-too-experienced poet, the hearing them sung by the wandering minstrels of the Dublin streets. Not seldom, it is to be feared, his warmth of heart prevented even these trivial gains from benefiting him, and like the "machine of pity" which his father had brought him up to be, he had parted with them to some importunate petitioner before he reached his home. Of his inconsiderate charity in this way a ludicrous anecdote is told. Once Edward Mills, coming to summon him to breakfast, was answered from within, that he must burst open the door, as his intended guest was unable to rise. He was, in fact, struggling to extricate himself from the ticking of his bed, into which, in the extreme cold, he had crawled, having surrendered his blankets to a poor woman who, on the preceding night, had vanquished him with a pitiful story.

On the 27th February, 1749, he was admitted to the degree of Bachelor of Arts, and his college days came to an end. One of the relics of this epoch, a *folio* Scapula, scrawled liberally with signatures and "promises to pay," was, in 1837, in the possession of his first biographer, Prior. He also left his autograph on one of the panes of No. 35. When, fifty years ago, the old garrets disappeared, this treasure was transferred to the manuscript room of Trinity College, where it remains. But perhaps the most significant memorial of his Dublin life is to be found in a passage from one of his later letters to his brother Henry. "The reasons you have given me for breeding up your son a scholar are judicious and convincing. . . . If he be assiduous, and divested of strong passions, (for passions in youth always lead to pleasure,) he may do very well in your college ; for it must be owned, that the industrious poor have good encouragement there, perhaps better than in any other in Europe. But if he has ambition, strong passions, and an exquisite sensibility of contempt, do not send him there, unless you have no other trade for him except your own."

CHAPTER II.

WHEN Oliver Goldsmith assembled his poor be-
longings, and took his last, and possibly regretful,
look at that scrawled signature on the window of No. 35
which was to become so precious a memento to posterity,
his prospects were of the most indefinite kind. His
father's death had broken up the old home at Lissoy;
and the house itself was now occupied by Mr. Hodson, to
whom the land had fallen in consequence of the arrange-
ments made by Charles Goldsmith for endowing his
daughter Catherine. Henry Goldsmith was domiciled in
the farm at Pallas, serving the curacy of Kilkenny West,
and teaching the village school. Mrs. Goldsmith, Oliver's
mother, had retired to a little cottage at Ballymahon,
and her circumstances were not such as enabled her to
support her son, especially as she had other children.
Obviously he must do something, but what? The
church appeared to afford the only practicable opening;
and he was urged by his relatives and his Uncle Contarine
to qualify for orders. To this proposal he had himself
strong objections. "To be obliged to wear a long wig,
when he liked a short one, or a black coat, when he
generally dressed in brown,"—he said afterwards in "The

Citizen of the World,"—was "a restraint upon his liberty." Perhaps also—to quote a reason he gave in later life for not reading prayers—he "did not think himself good enough." Yet he yielded to the importunity of those about him; and as he was too young to be ordained, agreed to make the needful preparations. "There is reason to believe," remarks Prior, gravely, "that at this time he followed no systematic plan of study." On the contrary, he seems to have occupied himself in a much more agreeable manner. From Ballymahon he wandered to Lissoy, from Lissoy to Pallas, from Pallas to Uncle Contarine's at Roscommon, leading, as Mr. Thackeray says, "the life of a buckeen," which is a minor form of "squireen," which again is the diminutive of 'squire. In most of its characteristics, his mode of existence must have resembled that of the typical eighteenth-century younger brother, Will Wimble. It was made up largely of journeyings from one house to another, of friendly fetching and carrying, of fishing and otter hunting in the isleted River Inny, of throwing the hammer at neighbouring fairs, of flute playing with his cousin, Jane Contarine, and, lastly, of taking the chair at the convivial meetings held nightly at one George Conway's Inn at Ballymahon. Here he was a triton among the minnows, the delight of horse doctors and bagmen, and the idol of his quondam college associate, Bob Bryanton, now of Ballymulvey. In days to come he would recur fondly to this disengaged, irresponsible time. It was of himself, not Tony Lumpkin, that he was thinking, when he attributed to that unlettered humourist the composition of the excellent drinking song in "She Stoops to Conquer." It was of himself, too, that he wrote—though his biographers have ignored the fact—when he makes him declare that he " always lov'd Cousin Con's hazel eyes, and her pretty long fingers, that she twists this way and that, over the haspicholls, like a parcel of bobbins." For who should " Cousin Con " be but Jane Contarine ?

There was, however, to be little romance of this kind in Oliver's chequered life. " Cousin Con " in time became Mrs. Lawder, and the inevitable hour at length arrived when the partner of her concerts must present himself for ordination to the Right Rev. Dr. Synge, Bishop of Elphin, by whom, sad to say, he was rejected. Whether, as is most probable, he had neglected the preliminary studies, whether the bishop had heard an ill report of his college career, or whether, as Dr. Strean asserted, he committed the solecism of appearing before his examiner in a pair of flaming scarlet breeches, are still debateable questions. The fact remains that he was refused acceptance as a clergyman, and must find a fresh vocation. Uncle Contarine, good at need, fitted him with a place as tutor to a gentleman of Roscommon of the name of Flinn. But he speedily, in consequence of the confinement, according to one account, in consequence of a quarrel about cards, according to another, relinquished this employ ; and, with thirty pounds of savings in his pocket, a circumstance which, to some extent, negatives the card story, quitted his mother's house on a good horse, and an uncertain errand. In about six weeks he re-appeared, without money, and having substituted for his roadster a miserable animal which he had christened contemptuously by the name of Fiddleback. His mode of departure had

been somewhat inconsiderate; his mode of returning was
eminently unsatisfactory, and Mrs. Goldsmith was naturally greatly incensed. Nor was she in any wise mollified
by his simple wonderment that, after all his struggles to get
home again, she was not more pleased to see him. His
brothers and sisters, however, effected a reconciliation;
and he afterwards wrote to his mother from Pallas a detailed account of his adventures. The letter, of which
Prior gives a copy, is believed to be authentic; but it is
more than suspected that romance has coloured the
narrative. He had gone to Cork, it says, sold his horse,
and taken a passage for America. But the ship sailed
without him when he was junketing in the country, and
he remained in Cork until he had but two guineas left.
Thereupon he had invested in "that generous beast,
Fiddleback," and turned Ballymahonwards with a re-
siduum of five shillings in his pocket, half of which
went promptly to a poor woman he met on the road.
He then proceeded to call upon a college friend, who
had often given him one of those warm general invita-
tions which are conventionally extended to unlikely
visitors. His host turned out to be a miser and a
valetudinarian, who shamelessly parodied Bishop Jewel
by recommending him to sell his horse, and purchase
a stout walking stick. While staying with this inhos-
pitable entertainer, he made the acquaintance of a
counsellor-at-law in the neighbourhood, "a man of
engaging aspect and polite address," who asked him to
dinner. "And now, my dear mother," the letter concludes, "I found sufficient to reconcile me to all my
follies; for here I spent three whole days. The

counsellor had two sweet girls to his daughters, who played enchantingly on the harpsichord ; and yet it was but a melancholy pleasure I felt the first time I heard them ; for that being the first time also that either of them had touched the instrument since their mother's death, I saw the tears in silence trickle down their father's cheeks. I every day endeavoured to go away, but every day was pressed and obliged to stay. On my going, the counsellor offered me his purse, with a horse and servant to convey me home ; but the latter I declined, and only took a guinea to bear my necessary expenses on the road." And thus he had arrived at Ballymahon.

The next step is thus briefly recounted by his sister, Mrs. Hodson. "His uncle Contarine, who was also reconciled to him, now resolved to send him to the Temple, that he might make the law his profession. But in his way to London, he met at Dublin with a sharper who tempted him to play, and emptied his pockets of fifty pounds, with which he had been furnished for his voyage and journey. He was obliged again to return to his poor mother, whose sorrow at his miscarriages need not be described, and his own distress and disgrace may readily be conceived." To this Prior adds that the sharper was a Roscommon acquaintance, and that Goldsmith continued some time in Dublin without daring to confess his loss. According to Mrs. Hodson, " he was again forgiven ; " but his mother, it appears, declined to receive him, and he took up his abode with his brother Henry. This last arrangement was interrupted by a quarrel, and in all probability most of the remaining time he spent in Ireland was passed with his long-suffering

Uncle Contarine. The old flute playing was resumed, and there are traditions that he occupied his leisure in the confection of more or less amatory lyrics for his " Cousin Con's " edification. But the time was fast approaching when he was to quit his Irish home for ever.

One of his relatives, a certain Dean Goldsmith of Cloyne, whose remarks were regarded in the family as oracular, occasionally visited Mr. Contarine, and this gentleman, struck by something that dropped from his young kinsman, was pleased to declare that he " would make an excellent medical man." This deliverance being considered decisive, another purse was contributed by Oliver's uncle, brother, and sister, and in the autumn of 1752 he set out once more to seek his elusive fortune. Upon this occasion he reached his destination, which was Edinburgh. His arrival there was nevertheless distinguished by a characteristic adventure. Having engaged a lodging, he set out at once to view the city, but having omitted to make any inquiries as to the name and locality of his new home, he was unable to find it again, and, but for an accidental meeting with the porter who had carried his baggage, must have begun his stay in Scotland with a fresh misfortune.

On January 13, 1753, he became a member of the Medical Society of Edinburgh, a voluntary association of the students, and he seems to have attended the lectures of Alexander Monro, the Professor of Anatomy, and of others. But the record of his social qualities, his tale-telling and his singing, is richer than the record of his studies. His first known piece of verse, exclusive of

the Æsop couplet, is an epigram called "The Clown's
Reply," dated "Edinburgh, 1753"; and one or two of
his letters to his friends have survived. He was not
a willing letter-writer. "An hereditary indolence (I have
it from the mother's side) has hitherto prevented my
writing to you," he says to Bob Bryanton, "and still
prevents my writing at least twenty-five letters more, due
to my friends in Ireland. No turnspit-dog gets up into
his wheel with more reluctance than I sit down to write;
yet no dog ever loved the roast meat he turns better
than I do him I now address." But already he exhibits
that delightful narrative ease which distinguishes "The
Citizen of the World," from which the following, with
its glimpse of the fair and hapless Duchess of Hamilton,
once Miss Elizabeth Gunning, might be an extract :—

"We have no such character here as a coquet, but alas!
how many envious prudes! Some days ago, I walked
into my Lord Kilcoubry's [Kirkcudbright's] (don't be
surprised, my lord is but a glover [1]) when the Duchess
of Hamilton (that fair who sacrificed her beauty to her
ambition, and her inward peace to a title and gilt
equipage) passed by in her chariot; her battered hus-
band, or more properly, the guardian of her charms, sat
by her side. Straight envy began, in the shape of no
less than three ladies who sat with me, to find faults
in her faultless form. 'For my part,' says the first, 'I
think, what I always thought, that the duchess has too

[1] "William Maclellan," says Prior, "who claimed the title, and
whose son succeeded in establishing the claim in 1773."

much of the red in her complexion.' 'Madam, I am
of your opinion,' says the second ; 'I think her face has
a palish cast, too much on the delicate order.' 'And
let me tell you,' added the third lady, whose mouth was
puckered up to the size of an issue, 'that the Duchess
has fine lips, but she wants a mouth.' At this every
lady drew up her mouth as if going to pronounce the
letter P.' "

One wonders whether Dickens recalled this passage,
when he drew that delightful mistress of the proprieties,
who expatiated upon the inestimable advantages to the
feminine lips of habitually pronouncing such words
as "prunes" and "prism." In two more letters
Goldsmith writes affectionately to his Uncle Contarine
of his professors and occupations, of a month's tour in
the Highlands on a horse "of about the size of a ram,"
and so forth. But he is already restlessly meditating
another move,—he proposes to go to Leyden to attend
the lectures of Albinus. From the latter of these two
epistles, his uncle's consent has been obtained, and he
is preparing to start, not for Leyden but for Paris,
"where the great Mr. Farhein, Petit, and Du Hamel du
Monceau instruct their pupils in all the branches of
medicine." "They speak French" [*i.e.*, in contradis-
tinction to the Latin of other continental professors], he
goes on, "and consequently I shall have much the
advantage of most of my countrymen, as I am perfectly
acquainted with that language, and few who leave
Ireland are so." From another passage in this letter,
he would seem to have been for some time an inmate

of, or rather visitor at, the Duke of Hamilton's house, but the allusion is obscure.

With these letters, and what of instruction may be extracted from a set of tailor's bills recovered by Forster, which show that "Mr. Oliver Goldsmith, Student," was helping to confirm the Elphin story of the red breeches by indulging in such "peacock's feathers" as "silver Hatt-Lace," "rich Sky-Blew sattin," "Genoa velvett" and "best sfine high Clarett-colour'd Cloth" at 19s. a yard, the record of his stay in the Scottish capital, as far as it can be chronicled in these pages, comes to an end. But he was not to quit the country, nor indeed to leave Edinburgh, without further adventures. His departure, according to the Percy Memoir, was all but prevented by his arrest for a debt contracted as surety for a friend. From this bondage, however, he was released by two college associates, Mr. Lauchlan Macleane and Dr. Sleigh. His subsequent experiences must be related in his own words to his Uncle Contarine, written from "Madame Diallion's, at Leyden," a few weeks later. "Sometime after the receipt of your last," he says, "I embarked for Bourdeaux, on board a Scotch ship called the St. Andrews, Capt. John Wall, master. The ship made a tolerable appearance, and as another inducement, I was let to know that six agreeable passengers were to be in my company. Well, we were but two days at sea when a storm drove us into a city of England called Newcastle-upon-Tyne. We all went a-shore to refresh us after the fatigue of our voyage. Seven men and I were one day on shore, and on the following evening as we were all very merry, the room door bursts open: enters a serjeant and twelve grenadiers with their bayonets screwed : and puts us all under the King's arrest. It seems my company were Scotchmen in the French service, and had been in Scotland to enlist soldiers for the French army. I endeavoured all I could to prove my innocence; however, I remained in prison with the rest a fortnight, and with difficulty got off even then. Dear Sir, keep all this a secret, or at least say it was for debt ; for if it were once known at the university, I should hardly get a degree. But hear how Providence interposed in my favour : the ship was gone on to Bourdeaux before I got from prison, and was wrecked at the mouth of the Garonne, and every one of the crew was drowned. It happened the last great storm. There was a ship at that time ready for Holland : I embarked, and in nine days, thank my God, I arrived safe at Rotterdam ; whence I travelled by land to Leyden ; and whence I now write."

As usual, a certain allowance must be made in this account for picturesque decoration. In the remainder of the letter he touches humourously on the contrast between the Dutch about him and the Scotch he has just left; describes the phlegmatic pleasures of the country, the ice-boats, and the delights of canal travelling. "They sail in covered boats drawn by horses," he says ; "and in these you are sure to meet people of all nations. Here the Dutch slumber, the French chatter, and the English play at cards. Any man who likes company may have them to his taste. For my part, I generally detached myself from all society, and was wholly taken up in observing the face of the country. Nothing can equal its beauty; wherever I turn my eye, fine houses,. elegant gardens, statues, grottos, vistas presented themselves; but when you enter their towns you are charmed beyond description. No misery is to be seen here; every one is usefully employed." Already, it is plain, he was insensibly storing up material for the subsequent " Traveller."

But the actual occurrences of his life are, for the moment, more urgent than his impressions of Holland. Little is known, in the way of fact, as to his residence at Leyden. Gaubius, the professor of chemistry, is indeed mentioned in one of his works; but it would be too much to conclude an intimacy from a chance reference. From the account of a fellow-countryman, Dr. Ellis, then a student like himself, he was, as always, frequently pressed for money, often supporting himself by teaching his native language, and now and then, in the hope of recruiting his finances, resorting to the gaming-table. On one occasion, according to this informant, he had a successful run; but, disregarding the advice of his friend to hold his ·hand, he lost his gains almost immediately. By and by the old restless longing to see foreign countries, probably dating from the days when he was a pupil under Thomas Byrne, came back with redoubled force. The recent death of the Danish savant and playwright, Baron de Holberg, who in his youth had made the tour of Europe on foot, probably suggested the way; and equipped with a small loan from Dr. Ellis, he determined to leave Leyden. Unhappily, in passing a florist's, he saw some rare bulbs, which he straightway transmitted to his Uncle Contarine.

His immediate resources being thus disposed of, he quitted Leyden in February, 1755, "with only one clean shirt and no money in his pocket."

His exact itinerary, once given verbally to Dr. Percy, is now undiscoverable. No letters of this date are known to exist. That he travelled on foot is clear. "*Haud inexpertus loquor*," he said later, when praising this method of locomotion; and Cooke, who wrote of him in *The European Magazine* for 1793, says he would often "with great pleasantry," speak "of his distresses on the Continent, such as living on the hospitalities of the friars in convents, sleeping in barns, and picking up a kind of mendicant livelihood by the German flute." "I had some knowledge of music"—says George Primrose in the "Vicar"—"with a tolerable voice, and now turned what was once my amusement into a present means of bare subsistence. I passed among the harmless peasants of Flanders, and among such of the French as are poor enough to be very merry; for I ever found them sprightly in proportion to their wants. Whenever I approached a peasant's house towards night-fall, I played one of my most merry tunes, and that procured me not only a lodging, but subsistence for the next day. I once or twice attempted to play for people of fashion; but they still thought my perform ance odious, and never rewarded me even with a trifle." For George Primrose we may read Oliver Goldsmith.

Louvain seems to have been his first tarrying place; and here, tradition affirms, he obtained that "authority to slay," the degree of M.B., later appended to his name. But the records of the University of Louvain were lost

in the wars of the Revolution, and the statement cannot
be verified. There are indications of his having been at
Antwerp, at Brussels, and at Maestricht. His musical
performances in France have already been referred to.
At Paris he attended the chemical lectures of the famous
Rouelle, for, in the "Polite Learning," he expressly speaks
of the number of ladies in the audience. His means of
subsistence at this time are involved in obscurity. It has
been asserted, although direct evidence is wanting, that
he acted as tutor or governor to an exceedingly miserly
young man of the middle classes; and there are passages
in George Primrose's after-experiences, which lend colour
to such a view. "I was to be the young gentleman's
governor, with this injunction, that he should always be
permitted to direct himself. My pupil in fact understood
the art of guiding in money concerns much better than
me. He was heir to a fortune of about two hundred
thousand pounds, left him by an uncle in the West
Indies; and his guardians, to qualify him for the
management of it, had bound him apprentice to an
attorney. Thus avarice was his prevailing passion: all
his questions on the road were how much money could
be saved. . . . Such curiosities on the way as could
be seen for nothing, he was ready enough to look at; but
if the sight was to be paid for, he usually asserted that he
had been told it was not worth seeing. He never
paid a bill, that he would not observe, how amazingly
expensive travelling was." But whether this is auto-
biographical, or not, Goldsmith must, in some way or
other, have procured money, since without it, he could
not have gone to the play, and seen the famous Mdlle.

Clairon, of whom he afterwards wrote so sympathetically in *The Bee.* From the French capital he passed to Germany; thence to Switzerland. It is at Geneva—at Voltaire's recently purchased residence of " Les Délices " —that Mr. Forster conjecturally places an incident which Goldsmith afterwards described in his memoirs of the philosopher of Ferney. " The person who writes this Memoir," he says, " who had the honour and pleasure of being his [Voltaire's] acquaintance, remembers to have seen him in a select company of wits of both sexes at Paris, when the subject happened to turn upon English taste and learning. Fontenelle, who was of the party, and who being unacquainted with the language or authors of the country he undertook to condemn, with a spirit truly vulgar began to revile both. Diderot, who liked the English, and knew something of their literary pretensions, attempted to vindicate their poetry and learning, but with unequal abilities. The company quickly perceived that Fontenelle was superior in the dispute, and were surprised at the silence which Voltaire had preserved all the former part of the night, particularly as the conversation happened to turn upon one of his favourite topics. Fontenelle continued his triumph till about twelve o'clock, when Voltaire appeared at last roused from his reverie. His whole frame seemed animated. He began his defence with the utmost elegance mixed with spirit, and now and then let fall the finest strokes of raillery upon his antagonist ; and his harangue lasted till three in the morning. I must confess that, whether from national partiality, or from the elegant sensibility of his manner, I never was so much charmed, nor did I ever remember so absolute a victory as he gained in this dispute." Goldsmith, it will be seen, places this occurrence at Paris, and, as one of his later editors, Mr. Gibbs, pertinently enough points out, the transference of the scene to "Les Délices" involves the not very explicable presence in Switzerland of Diderot and Fontenelle, to say nothing of the "select company of wits ot both sexes." But these discrepancies, due to haste, to confusion, or perhaps to the habit, already referred to, of "loading" his narrative, do not make it necessary to conclude that Goldsmith had *not* seen and heard Voltaire.

In Switzerland Goldsmith remained some time, chiefly at Geneva, visiting from thence Basle, Berne, and other places. He speaks, in the "Animated Nature," of woodcocks flushed on Mount Jura, of a frozen cataract seen at Schaffhausen, of a "very savoury dinner" eaten on the Alps. Later, he passed into Piedmont, and makes reference to its floating bee-houses. Florence, Verona, Mantua, Milan, Venice, were next journeyed to, and Padua, for which city is also claimed the credit of his medical degree. In Italy, where every peasant was a musician, his flute had lost its charm, and he seems to have subsisted, if we again accept him as the prototype of George Primrose, chiefly by disputation. "In all the foreign universities and convents, there are upon certain days philosophical theses maintained against every adventitious disputant; for which, if the champion opposes with any dexterity, he can claim a gratuity in money, a dinner, and a bed for one night." Thus he fought his way from city to city until, at the end of 1755, he turned his steps homewards. On the 1st of February, 1756, he landed at Dover, "his whole stock of cash," says Glover, "amounting to no more than a few half-pence." His wanderings had occupied exactly one year.

CHAPTER III.

AT the time of Goldsmith's second arrival in England, for, as will be remembered, he had already paid an unpremeditated visit to Newcastle a year earlier, his previous career could certainly not be described as a success. If his schooldays had been but moderately promising, his college life might almost be called discreditable. He had tried many things and failed. He had estranged his sole remaining parent; he had sorely taxed the patience of the rest of his relations; and he had, latterly, been living as a wanderer on the face of the earth. This was his record in the past. And yet, read by the light of his subsequent story, he had unconsciously gone through a course of training, and accumulated a stock of experience, of which little or nothing was to be lost. He had looked at sorrow close, and learned to sympathize with poverty; he had known men and cities; he had studied character in its undress. If he had profited but slenderly by the precepts of Gaubius and Albinus, his "education through the senses" had been progressing as silently and as surely as the fame of Marcellus. What he had seen of foreign countries was to stand him in good stead in his first long poem; what he had collected con-

cerning professors and academies he would weave into
the "Enquiry into Polite Learning in Europe"; what he
had observed in the byway and the crowd would supply
him with endless touches of shrewd and delicate dis-
crimination in his "Essays" and his "Citizen of the
World." And somehow, he had already, as his letters
testify, acquired that easy and perspicuous style of writing,
which comes to few men as a gift. Who shall say, then,
that his life had been a failure, when, in its assimilative
period, so much had been achieved? Meanwhile, he
had landed at Dover, and the world was all before him
where to choose.

The close connection between his works and his
biography, added to the habit of regarding the adventures of his "Philosophic Vagabond" as an exact transcript of his own experiences, has occasionally led to the
including, in that biography, of some incidents which
may have no other basis than his fictions. Thus, either
from his subsequent account, in *The British Magazine*,
of the vicissitudes of a strolling player, or from the
theatrical attempts of George Primrose in the "Vicar,"
it has been asserted that his first endeavour at what he
somewhere calls "his sole ambition, a livelihood," was as
a low comedian in a barn—an assertion which has been
thought to receive some slender confirmation from the
fact that he is known to have expressed a desire in later
life to play the part of "Scrub" in Farquhar's "Beaux
Stratagem." Another vaguely reported story represents
him as engaged for some time as usher at a provincial
school, under a feigned name: and that his difficulties,
during this period, were extreme, may be gathered from

the oft-quoted, but perhaps humourously-exaggerated, announcement, attributed to him in his more prosperous days, that he had once lived "among the beggars in Axe-Lane." In any case he must have been sorely pressed, and depressed. " I was without friends, recommendations, money, or impudence," he says to his brother-in-law Hodson, writing of this time; "and that in a country where being born an Irishman was sufficient to keep me unemployed. Many in such circumstances would have had recourse to the friar's cord, or the suicide's halter. But, with all my follies, I had principle to resist the one, and resolution to combat the other." His first definite employment seems to have been that of assistant to an apothecary named Jacob on Fish Street Hill, who had been attracted by his chemical knowledge, and pitied his forlorn condition. While he was acting in this capacity, he heard that his quondam college friend, Dr. Sleigh, already referred to in chapter ii., was in London, and he accordingly sought him out. "Notwithstanding it was Sunday," said poor Goldsmith to Cooke, "and it is to be supposed in my best clothes, Sleigh scarcely knew me—such is the tax the unfortunate pay to poverty—however, when he did recollect me, I found his heart as warm as ever, and he shared his purse and friendship with me during his continuance in London."

By the kindness of Dr. Sleigh, and some other friends, he was freed from the pestle and mortar, and established himself as "a physician in a humble way " in Bankside, Southwark, where, if anywhere, he must have made the acquaintance of that worshipful Madame Blaize, whom, three years later, he celebrated in *The Bee*. " Kent Street," he sings—

> " well may say
> That had she lived a twelvemonth more
> She had not died to-day ; "

and Kent Street, then sacred to beggars and broom men, traverses Southwark.[1] His old schoolmate, Beatty, who saw him about this time, described him as conventionally costumed in tarnished green and gold, but with a "shirt and neckcloth which appeared to have been worn at least a fortnight. He said he was practising physic, and doing very well." Another story, told or repeated by Reynolds, also relates to the—in Goldsmith's life—always important item of attire. "In conformity to the prevailing garb of the day for physicians," says Prior, "Goldsmith, unable probably to obtain a new, had procured a second-hand, velvet coat ; but either from being deceived in the bargain or by subsequent accident, a considerable breach in the left breast was obliged to be repaired by the introduction of a new piece. This had not been so neatly done, as not to be apparent to the close observation of his acquaintance, and such persons as he visited in the capacity of medical attendant : willing, therefore, to conceal what is considered too obvious a symptom of poverty, he was accustomed to place his hat over the patch, and retain it there carefully during the visit ; but this constant position becoming noticed, and the cause being soon known, occasioned no little merriment at his expense."

His statement to Beatty, quoted above, that he was prospering, was, in all probability, what he himself would have described as " a bounce." His patients were of the poorest class, and the neighbourhood in which he

[1] It is now called Tabard Street.

"practised physic" one of the least opulent in London.
Hence he soon drifted into new employment. Rumour
affirms that, through one of his humble patients, a
working printer, he made the acquaintance of the
author of "Clarissa," Samuel Richardson, whose shop
was in Salisbury Court, and that he acted for him as
corrector to the press. This quasi-literary occupation
must have revived or stimulated his leaning to author-
ship; for when, about this time, he called upon another
Edinburgh acquaintance, he had exchanged his tarnished
gold and green for " a rusty full-trimmed black suit,"
the pockets of which were crammed with papers, sug-
gesting "the poet in Garrick's farce of 'Lethe.'"
To complete the resemblance, he speedily produced a
tragedy, which he insisted upon reading, hastily blotting
out everything to which his listener offered the faintest
objection. At last he let out that he had already submitted it to Richardson, upon which his friend, doubtful
of his own critical abilities, and alarmed for the possible
fate of a masterpiece, " peremptorily declined offering
another criticism upon the performance," the very name
and subject of which have perished, like those of the
comedy Steele burned at Oxford in deference to the
objections of Mr. Parker. As usual, Goldsmith was
brimful of projects, one of which was to start there and
then for the East in order to decipher the inscriptions on
the Wady Mekatteb and the Djebal Seibal. For this a
salary of £300 per annum had been left by an enthusiast;
and nothing was needful but the knowledge of Arabic—
a mere "unconsidered trifle" that could easily be picked
up on the road.

The famous "Written Mountains," however, were not to be his destination. Another of his old Edinburgh class-fellows—and it is noteworthy that there were so many who seem to have remembered and befriended him—was the son of Dr. Milner, a Presbyterian minister and schoolmaster at Peckham. Dr. Milner was in failing health, and his son suggested that Goldsmith should, for the time, act as his assistant. Whether the sarcastic comments upon the miseries of an usher's position, to which he gives vent in *The Bee*, the "Vicar," and elsewhere, are referable to this period, or to some less fortunate experiences, is still unchronicled. But there is certainly a touch of something more than a merely dramatic utterance in the phrases of George Primrose: "I have been an usher at a boarding-school myself; and may I die by an anodyne necklace,[1] but I had rather be an under turnkey in Newgate. I was up early and late: I was brow-beat by the master, hated for my ugly face by the mistress, worried by the boys within, and never permitted to stir out to meet civility abroad." "Every trick," he says again in No. vi. of *The Bee*, "is played upon the usher; the oddity of his manners, his dress, or his language, are [is] a fund of eternal ridicule ; the master himself now and then cannot avoid joining in the laugh, and the poor wretch, eternally resenting this ill-usage, seems to live in a state of war with all the family." At other times, says the "Percy Memoir," he would describe the malodorous privileges of sleeping in the same bed with the French teacher, who spends

---

[1] That is, by a halter, for which, by extension, the name of the old quack remedy for the pains of teething was employed.

" every night an hour perhaps in papering and filleting his hair, and stinks worse than a carrion, with his rancid pomatums, when he lays his head beside him on his bolster." But if these indignities lingered in his mind, (and the passages in *The Bee* must have been written very shortly after his Peckham experiences), he can have discovered little of his annoyance to those about him, who seem to have recollected him chiefly by his improvidence,—a characteristic so manifest that Mrs. Milner is said to have suggested that she should take care of his money like that of the young gentlemen, —his good-nature, his cheerfulness, his playing upon the flute to his pupils, and his practical jokes upon William the foot-boy. Such, at all events, is the impression left by the reminiscences of the last of the ten Miss Milners who survived until the close of the century to enlighten curious inquirers concerning her father's famous assistant. The limits of this volume do not permit the reproduction of Goldsmith's tricks upon the unsuspecting William, who must certainly have been a gull of the first order ; but two incidents of these days may be recorded, because they illustrate the permanent side of Goldsmith's nature. According to tradition, it occurred to Miss Hester Milner who, it must be remembered, was the daughter of a minister, to inquire what particular commentator on the Scriptures he would recommend, upon which he replied, after a pause, and with much earnestness, that in his belief the best commentator was common-sense. The other anecdote, which Prior derived from the son of one of the boys who was present, is allied to those earlier ones which exhibit his character in its more vulnerable aspect. Playing the flute one day to his pupils, he paused for a moment to expatiate upon the advantages of music as a gentlemanlike acquirement. "A pert boy, looking at his situation and personal disadvantages with something of contempt, rudely replied to the effect that *he* surely could not consider himself a gentleman ; an offence which, though followed by instant chastisement, disconcerted and pained him extremely." It was probably owing to slights of this kind that, although he left so satisfactory an impression behind him, he always looked back to the days of this servitude with unusual bitterness. He would talk freely of his distresses and difficulties, Cooke tells us, but he always carefully avoided the "little story of Peckham school."

His stay there, however, can have been but brief. Miss Milner, indeed, talked of a three years' residence ; but, if Forster be right in fixing his entry upon his duties at "about the beginning of 1757," it could scarcely have exceeded three months, as it is possible to fix definitely the termination of the engagement. Dr. Milner was a dabbler in literature, and a contributor to *The Monthly Review*, which, a few years earlier, had been established by Griffiths the bookseller. Griffiths was thus an occasional visitor at Peckham, and, struck by some remark on the part of the usher, he called him aside and inquired whether he could furnish "a few specimens of criticism." These, when prepared, were so satisfactory, that an agreement was entered into in April by which Goldsmith was to be released from Peckham, to have a fixed salary,—qualified indifferently by Percy as "handsome," by Prior as "adequate," and by Forster as "small,"—and to prepare copy-of-all-work for his master's periodical.

Griffiths' shop was in Paternoster Row—"at the Sign of the Dunciad." Most of the mere paste-and-scissors work of the magazine was done by the bookseller himself, the criticisms being supplied by a staff which included several contemporary writers of minor rank. Ruffhead, who wrote a life of Pope, Kippis, of the "Biographia Britannica," James Grainger, afterwards the poet of "The Sugar Cane," and Langhorne, one of the transla- tors of Plutarch's "Lives," were amongst these, to whose number Goldsmith must now be added. In Griffiths' copy of the review for this period, which once belonged to Richard Heber, his new assistant's articles were marked, so that it is possible to form some idea of the very miscellaneous nature of his duties. He reviewed the "Mythology and Poetry of the Celtes," by Mallet of Copenhagen; he reviewed Home's "Douglas" and Burke "On the Sublime and Beautiful;" he reviewed the new "History of England" by Smollett and tea- hating old Jonas Hanway's "Eight Days' Journey from Portsmouth to Kingston-upon-Thames." "Letters from an Armenian in Ireland, to his Friends at Trebi- sonde "—concerning which it is quite competent for any one to assert that they suggested the subsequent "Citizen of the World," were it not that such collections appear to have been in the air at the time—a translation of Cardinal Polignac's "Anti-Lucretius," Wilkie's "Epi- goniad," and the "Memoirs of Madame de Maintenon," are also among the heterogeneous list. One of the last of his efforts for the review was a notice of Gray's

"Odes," which Dodsley had just published in a shilling *quarto*. It is interesting, because it shows how, in his long probation, his taste had gradually been formed. He admitted Gray's genius ; he admitted his exquisite verbal felicities ; but he regretted his remoteness, and his want of emotion, and he gave him the advice of Isocrates to his scholars,—to "study the people." Counsel from the back-parlour of the "Dunciad" to the cloistered precinct of Pembroke College was not likely to be much regarded, even if it reached that sanctuary of culture ; but the fact illustrates the difference between Gray and the writer of whom he was afterwards to say, "This man is a poet."

Goldsmith's criticism of Gray appeared in *The Monthly Review* for September, 1757, and at this point his labours for Griffiths were interrupted. The reasons for this are obscure; but incompatibility of temper may probably stand for all of them. It is not unlikely that Goldsmith's habits were too desultory and uncertain to suit an employer with confirmed business habits, and a low standard of literary excellence ; while Goldsmith, on his side, complained that the bookseller and his wife (who assisted him) not only denied him the requisite comforts, but edited and manipulated his articles,—always a thing intolerable to the possessor of an individual style. Style, however, was little to honest Griffiths, who doubtless thought, not without some reason, that he knew better what he wanted than the unknown Peckham usher whom he had introduced into the world of letters. So Griffiths and his assistant dissolved their compact, the latter to live for the next few months, no one quite knows how, by miscellaneous practice of the pen.[1] His brother Charles, attracted from Ireland by some romancing phrases in one of his elder's letters about his illustrious friends, visited him unexpectedly at the end of 1757. To his disappointment, he found him in a squalid garret near Salisbury Square, and promptly recognizing the improbability of help in this direction, vanished as suddenly as he came.

But if there is uncertainty as to Goldsmith's general occupations at this time, there is one work upon which, either during his bondage in Paternoster Row, or immediately after, he must have been engaged. This was a translation of the remarkable Memoirs of Jean Marteilhe of Bergerac, which Griffiths and Dilly published in February, 1758, under the title of " Memoirs of a Protestant Condemned to the Galleys of France for his Religion." The book, it is true, " from prudential motives " now no longer very intelligible, bears the name of James Willington, an old class-fellow of Goldsmith at Trinity College. But Griffiths, according to Prior, acknowledged that the translator was Goldsmith himself. Indeed, it is not impossible that Goldsmith may have seen Marteilhe, who died at Cuylenberg as late as 1777, and, who, the preface expressly says, was, at the time of writing, " known to numbers, not only in Holland, but London." Of late years the Religious Tract Society has issued a somewhat exacter version of this moving record, surely one of the

---

[1] Mr. J. W. M. Gibbs (Goldsmith's " Works," Bell's edition, vol. v.) has discovered that some parts of " A History of the Seven Years' War," hitherto supposed to have been written in 1761, were published in *The Literary Magazine*, 1757-8.

most forcible pictures of the miseries ensuing upon the Revocation of the Edict of Nantes that has ever been penned, and not wholly undeserving the praise accorded to it by Michelet of seeming to have been "written as if between earth and heaven." Nor, despite certain apologetic passages in the translator's preface, can it be held to be seriously deficient in romantic interest. The episode of Goujon, the young cadet of the regiment of Aubesson, and the disastrous development of his love-story, might furnish ample material for one of Dumas' most stirring chapters.

By the time, however, that the "Memoirs of a Protestant" had appeared, Goldsmith had deserted his garret near Salisbury Square, and gone back to help Dr. Milner at Peckham. Here, at least, he found a home, added to which, his old master had promised to endeavour to procure for him a medical appointment in India. With a view to the necessary outfit, he seems to have set about what was to be his first original work, and his letters to his friends in Ireland, of which several written at this time were printed by Prior and Percy, are plainly prompted by the desire to obtain subscribers. He is going to publish a book in London, he says to Edward Mills, "entitled An Essay on the Present State of Taste and Literature in Europe," and he goes on to beg him to circulate proposals for the same. To like effect he writes to Robert Bryanton, and to Jane Contarine, now Mrs. Lawder. These letters are excellent specimens of his epistolary art. All written within a few days of each other, they are skilfully discriminate in their variation of style. To Mills, who, by the way, never answered his appeal, he is most formal ; he is addressing the rich relation, the well-to-do " squireen," who had patronised him at college. " I have often," he says, " let my fancy loose when you were the subject, and have imagined you gracing the bench, or thundering at the bar ; while I have taken no small pride to myself, and whispered all that I could come near, that this was my cousin. Instead of this, it seems you are contented to be merely an happy man ; to be esteemed only by your acquaintance—to cultivate your paternal acres—to take unmolested a nap under one of your own hawthorns, or in Mrs. Mills' bedchamber, which, even a poet must confess, is rather the most [more] comfortable place of the two." Already, it will be seen, he speaks of himself as a " poet." To Bryanton he writes with the freedom of an ancient boon companion at the Three Pigeons, runs over their old experiences, deplores their enforced separation, and draws a half-humorous, half-bitter picture of his own neglected merits. " There will come a day," he says, " no doubt it will—I beg you may live a couple of hundred years longer only to see the day—when the Scaligers and Daciers will vindicate my character, give learned editions of my labours, and bless the times with copious comments on the text. You shall see how they will fish up the heavy scoundrels who disregard me now, or will then offer to cavil at my productions. How will they bewail the time that suffered so much genius to be neglected. If ever my works find their way to Tartary or China, I know the consequence. Suppose one of your Chinese Owanowitzers instructing one of your Tartarian Chianobacchi—you see I use Chinese names to show my

own erudition, as I shall soon make our Chinese talk like
an Englishman to show his. This may be the subject
of the lecture :—

" 'Oliver Goldsmith flourished in the eighteenth and
nineteenth centuries. He lived to be an hundred and
three years old [and in that] age may justly be styled
the sun of [literature] and the Confucius of Europe.
[Many of his earlier writings to the regret of the] learned
world were anonymous, and have probably been lost,
because united with those of others. The first avowed
piece the world has of his is entitled an "Essay on the
Present State of Taste and Literature in Europe,"—a
work well worth its weight in diamonds. In this he
profoundly explains what learning is, and what learning
is not. In this he proves that blockheads are not men
of wit, and yet that men of wit are actually blockheads.' " [1]

And then—not "to tire his Chinese Philosopher,"
of whom, two or three years hence, we shall hear more
in *The Public Ledger*—he "lights down, as the boys say,
to see himself on horse-back," and where is he ? "Here
in a garret writing for bread, and expecting to be
dunned for a milk-score."

The letter to Mrs. Lawder—Cousin Con. of the
harpsichords—is in a different strain from the two others.
Half playful, half respectful, it is at the same time more
personal and confidential. After explaining his long
silence by his fears that his letters might be attributed

---

[1] The words between square brackets were supplied by Prior, the
original manuscript being, in these places, worn by age.

to wrong motives—that is to say, to petitions for money
—he goes on :—

"Those who know me at all, know that I have always
been actuated by different principles from the rest of
Mankind, and while none regarded the interests of his
friends more, no man on earth regarded his own less.
I have often affected bluntness to avoid the imputation
of flattery, have frequently seem'd to overlook those
merits, too obvious to escape notice, and pretended
disregard to those instances of good nature and good
sense which I could not fail tacitly to applaud; and all
this lest I should be rank'd among the grinning
tribe who say very true to all that is said, who fill a
vacant chair at a tea table whose narrow souls never
moved in a wider circle than the circumference of a
guinea, and who had rather be reckoning the money
in your pocket than the virtues of your breast; all this,
I say, I have done and a thousand other very silly
tho' very disinterested things in my time, and for all
which no soul cares a farthing about me. . . . Madam,
is it to be wondered that he should once in his life
forget you who has been all his life forgetting himself?

"However it is probable you may one of these days
see me turn'd into a perfect Hunks and as dark and
intricate as a mouse-hole. I have already given my
Lanlady orders for an entire reform in the state of my
finances; I declaim against hot suppers, drink less
sugar in my tea, and cheek my grate with brick-bats.
Instead of hanging my room with pictures I intend to
adorn it with maxims of frugality, these will make

pretty furniture enough, and won't be a bit too expensive; for I shall draw them all out with my own hands and my lanlady's daughter shall frame them with the parings of my black waistcoat; Each maxim is to be inscrib'd on a sheet of clean paper and wrote with my best pen, of which the following will serve as a specimen. ' Look Sharp. Mind the mean chance. Money is money now. If you have a thousand pounds you can put your hands by your sides and say you are worth a thousand pounds every day of the year. Take a farthing from an hundred pound and it will be an hundred pound no longer.' Thus which way so ever I turn my eyes they are sure to meet one of those friendly Monitors, and as we are told of an Actor [1] who hung his room round with looking-glasses to correct the defects of his person, my appartment shall be furnishd in a peculiar manner to correct the errors of my mind.

" Faith, Madam, I heartily wish to be rich, if it were only for this reason, to say without a blush how much I esteem you, but alass I have many a fatigue to encounter before that happy time comes; when your poor old simple friend may again give a loose to the luxuriance of his nature, sitting by Kilmore fireside recount the various adventures of an hard fought life, laugh over the follies of the day, join his flute to your harpsicord and forget that ever he starv'd in those streets where Butler and Otway starv'd before him." [2]

[1] *I.e.*, Thomas Sheridan, the father of the author of "The School for Scandal."

[2] This extract is printed textually from a *facsimile* of the original letter in Griffin's " Works of Oliver Goldsmith," 1858.

And so, with a pathetic reference to his kind Uncle Contarine, now lapsed into "second childishness and mere oblivion," he winds into the business of his letter —the solicitation of subscriptions for the forthcoming book.

Three months after the date of this epistle the long-desired appointment has come, and he describes it to his brother-in-law Hodson. He is going in quality of physician and surgeon to a factory on the Coast of Coromandel. The Company have signed the warrant, which has already cost £10, and there will be other heavy expenses for passage and outfit. The salary of £100, it is true, is only trifling. Still the practice of the place (if he is rightly informed), "generally amounts to not less than £1,000 per annum, for which the appointed physician has an exclusive privilege." An East India exile, however, was not to be his fate. Why the project, with its executed warrant, and boundless potentialities, came to nothing, his biographers have failed to discover, nor did he himself ever reveal the reason. But in the absence of information upon this point, there is definite evidence upon another. In December of the same year, 1758, he presented himself at Surgeons' Hall to be examined for the humble office of hospital mate. The curt official record in the College books, first made public by Prior, runs as follows :—

"James Bernard, mate to an hospital. OLIVER GOLD-SMITH, found not qualified for ditto."

CHAPTER IV.

BY this date Goldsmith had passed that critical time
of life, after which, according to a depressing French
axiom, whose falsity he was to demonstrate, no man that has
hitherto failed can hope to succeed. His thirtieth birth-
day had gone by. In a letter written not many weeks
after the disaster which closed the foregoing chapter,
he gives a description of his appearance at the beginning
of 1759. " Though I never had a day's sickness since
I saw you, yet I am not that strong active man you once
knew me. You scarcely can conceive how much eight
years of disappointment, anguish, and study have worn
me down. . . . Imagine to yourself a pale melancholy
visage, with two great wrinkles between the eyebrows,
with an eye disgustingly severe, and a big wig; and you
may have a perfect picture of my present appearance.
. . . . I have passed my days among a parcel of cool
designing beings, and have contracted all their suspicious
manner in my own behaviour. I should actually be as
unfit for the society of my friends at home, as I detest
that which I am obliged to partake of here. . . . I can
neither laugh nor drink, have contracted an hesitating
disagreeable manner of speaking, and a visage that looks
ill-nature itself; in short, I have thought myself into a

settled melancholy, and an utter disgust of all that life brings with it." That this picture is strongly coloured by the depression of the moment is manifest. " Never," says Percy, commenting upon part of it, "was a character so unsuspicious and so unguarded as the writer's." But the life he had led was not calculated to soften his manners or modify his physical disadvantages.

About the end of 1758,—and probably, as Mr. Forster conjectures, with part of the money he had received for some articles in *The Critical Review* of Griffiths' rival, Hamilton,—Goldsmith had moved from his Salisbury Square garret into his now historic lodgings in Green Arbour Court. Green Arbour Court was a tiny square, which extended from the upper end of the Old Bailey into Sea-coal Lane, and was approached on that side by a steep flight of stone stairs (of which Ned Ward has chronicled the dangers) called Breakneck Steps. When Washington Irving visited it, before its demolition, he described it as a region of washerwomen, consisting of " tall and miserable houses, the very intestines of which seemed turned inside out, to judge from the old garments and frippery that fluttered from every window." In *The European Magazine* for January, 1803, the reader may see a contemporary print of the place, still to be identified on ancient maps of London. Goldsmith's room was on the first floor at No. 12 ; and here, solaced by the humours of a friendly watchmaker, or recreating the ragged infantry of the neighbourhood with his flute, working busily in the daytime, and creeping out stealthily at nightfall, he made his home from 1758 until the end of 1760.

The first months of his residence were signalized by one of those untoward incidents, which are always a difficulty to the hero-worshipping biographer. In order to make a decent appearance before the Court of Examiners at Surgeons' Hall, he had applied to Griffiths to become security with a tailor for a suit of clothes, and, upon his promising to write four articles for *The Monthly Review*, Griffiths had consented. The reviews had been written, and the examination undergone, with the result already recorded, when Goldsmith's landlord at Green Arbour Court was suddenly arrested for debt. To comfort his inconsolable wife, Goldsmith pledged the clothes. A few days later, under further pressure, the books he had reviewed were transferred to a friend as security for a small loan; and by ill luck, almost immediately afterwards, the irate Griffiths demanded restitution. Thereupon ensued a bitter and humiliating correspondence, the closing letter in which was printed by Mr. Forster from the original in his possession. It is a passionate outburst on Goldsmith's part, in which he almost implores the bookseller to send him to prison. He has told him again and again, he can pay him nothing; but he will be punctual to any arrangement made. He is not a sharper (as Griffiths had evidently called him); had he been so, had he been possessed of less good nature and native generosity, he might surely now have been in better circumstances. " I am guilty, I own," he says, " of meannesses which poverty unavoidably brings with it, my reflections are filled with repentance for my imprudence, but not with any remorse for being a villain." The volumes reviewed, which are merely in the custody of a friend, shall be returned in a month. "At least spare invective 'till my book with Mr. Dodsley shall be publish'd, and then perhaps you may see the bright side of a mind when my professions shall not appear the dictates of necessity but of choice." Thus, without let or break, in a hand trembling with agitation and wounded pride, the words hurry on to the postscript, " I shall expect impatiently the result of your resolutions." The result seems to have been that Griffiths refrained from further proceedings ; and the matter ended with an engagement on Goldsmith's part to prepare, for twenty pounds, from which the price of the clothes was to be deducted, a " Life of Voltaire," to accompany a new translation of " The Henriade " by one of the bookseller's hacks.

To this work, already quoted, he refers in the letter to Henry Goldsmith of February, 1759, containing the personal portrait with which the present chapter opens. After mentioning his mother, who by this time has become almost blind, sending affectionate injunctions to Bob Bryanton not to drink, and making brotherly inquiries after his younger sister Jenny, who has married ill, he goes on :—

" There is a book of mine will be published in a few days, the life of a very extraordinary man—no less than the great Voltaire. You know already by the title, that it is no more than a catch-penny. However I spent but four weeks on the whole performance, for which I received twenty pounds. When published, I shall take some means of conveying it to you, unless you may think it dear of [at] the postage, which may amount

to four or five shillings. However, I fear you will not
find an equivalence of amusement. Your last letter, I
repeat it, was too short; you should have given me your
opinion of the heroicomical poèm which I sent you:
you remember I intended to introduce the hero of the
poem, as lying in a paltry alehouse. You may take the
following specimen of the manner, which I flatter myself
is quite original. The room in which he lies, may be
described somewhat this way :—

> " ' The window, patch'd with paper, lent a ray,
> That feebly shew'd the state in which he lay.
> The sanded floor, that grits beneath the tread :
> The humid wall with paltry pictures spread ;
> The game of goose was there exposed to view,
> And the twelve rules the royal martyr drew :
> The seasons fram'd with listing, found a place,
> And Prussia's monarch shew'd his lampblack face.
> The morn was cold ; he views with keen desire,
> A rusty grate unconscious of a fire.
> An unpaid reck'ning on the freeze was scor'd,
> And five crack'd tea-cups dress'd the chimney board.

"And now imagine after his soliloquy, the landlord to
make his appearance, in order to dun him for the reckoning :—

> " ' Not with that face, so servile and so gay,
> That welcomes every stranger that can pay ;
> With sulky eye he smoak'd the patient man,
> Then pull'd his breeches tight, and thus began, &c.'

"All this is taken, you see, from nature. It is a good
remark of Montaign's, that the wisest men often have
friends, with whom they do not care how much they play

the fool. Take my present follies as instances of regard. Poetry is a much easier, and more agreeable species of composition than prose, and could a man live by it, it were not unpleasant employment to be a poet."

Honest Henry Goldsmith, in his remote Irish curacy, might perhaps be excused from offering any critical opinions upon a fragment, the ultimate development of which it was so little possible to forecast. The author himself seems to have carried it no farther than this introductory description, some details of which are certainly borrowed from his own Green Arbour Court environment. It was still a fragment when later he worked it into letter xxix. of "The Citizen of the World;" and when, in 1770, part of it served for the decoration of "The Deserted Village," it had found its final use. But it is interesting as being, with exception of the trifling epigram written in Scotland in 1753, and already referred to in chapter ii., the first poetical utterance of Goldsmith concerning which there is definite evidence. From this alone, as the production of a poet of thirty-one, it would be hard to predict "The Traveller" or "Retaliation." Certainly, as Johnson said, Goldsmith "was a plant that flowered late."

Not long after the date of the above letter to Henry Goldsmith, Breakneck Steps were scaled by an illustrious inquirer, whose experiences are, with becoming mystery, related in the "Percy Memoir." "A friend of his," says that record, in some respects the most important account that exists concerning Goldsmith, "paying him a visit at the beginning of March, 1759, found him in lodgings there so poor and uncomfortable, that he should not think it proper to mention the circumstance, if he did not consider it as the highest proof of the splendor of Dr. Goldsmith's genius and talents, that by the bare exertion of their powers, under every disadvantage of person and fortune, he could gradually emerge from such obscurity to the enjoyment of all the comforts and even luxuries of life, and admission into the best societies in London. The Doctor was writing his Enquiry, &c., in a wretched dirty room, in which there was but one chair, and when he, from civility, offered it to his visitant, himself was obliged to sit in the window. While they were conversing, some one gently rapped at the door, and being desired to come in, a poor little ragged girl of very decent behaviour, entered, who, dropping a curtsie, said, 'My mamma sends her compliments, and begs the favour of you to lend her a chamber-pot full of coals.'"

The visitor here mentioned so reticently was Percy himself, not yet Bishop of Dromore, but only chaplain to Lord Sussex and Vicar of Easton Mauduit in Northamptonshire. He had been introduced to Goldsmith by Grainger of *The Monthly Review*, at the Temple Exchange Coffee House; and, as he was already collecting the materials for his "Reliques of English Poetry," had no doubt been attracted by his new friend's knowledge of ballad literature. He was wrong, however, in thinking that Goldsmith was writing the "Enquiry," of which he must rather have been correcting the proofs, as it was published for the Dodsleys in the following April.

It is a commonplace to say that the "Enquiry into the Present State of Polite Learning in Europe" was somewhat over-titled. In the first edition it is but a small and not very closely printed *duodecimo* of two hundred pages ; and it is shorter still in the revised issue of 1774, from which a considerable portion, and notably much of the chapter relating to the stage, was withdrawn. Obviously so wide a survey could scarcely be confined in so narrow a space. Nor, with all his gifts, was Goldsmith sufficiently equipped for the task. It is true he had travelled upon the Continent (his sketch, he says, though general, "was for the most part taken upon the spot"), and he was right in claiming certain advantages for the pedestrian's point of view. "A man who is whirled through Europe in a postchaise, and the pilgrim who walks the grand tour on foot, will form very different conclusions," he affirms, adding, with a frankness confined to the first edition, "*Haud inexpertus loquor.*" But he forgot that there is also something to be said for the rival mode of locomotion, and that it may be urged that the one he adopted is open to the charge of being too exclusively that of an outsider. It is needless, however, to cross-question closely the agreement of Goldsmith's performance with his promise. What attracted him most, as Mr. Forster has not failed to point out, was less the condition of letters in Europe than the condition of letters in the immediate neighbourhood of his retreat in the Old Bailey. The mercantile avidity and sordid standards of the bookseller, the venal rancour of the hungry critics in his pay, the poverty of the poets, the decay of patronage, the slow rewards of genius, all these were nearer to his heart (and vision) than the learning of Luitprandus, or the "philological performances " of Constantinus Afer. Some of his periods, indeed, have almost a note of personal disclosure. Who shall say, for example, that, in more than one sentence of the following, it was not Oliver Goldsmith whom he had in mind? " If the author be, therefore, still so necessary among us, let us treat him with proper consideration, as a child of the public, not a rent-charge on the community. And, indeed, a *child* of the public he is in all respects ; for while so well able to direct others, how incapable is he frequently found of guiding himself. His simplicity exposes him to all the insidious approaches of cunning, his sensibility to the slightest invasions of contempt. Though possessed of fortitude to stand unmoved the expected bursts of an earthquake, yet of feelings so exquisitely poignant as to agonize under the slightest disappointment. Broken rest, tasteless meals, and causeless anxiety, shorten his life, or render it unfit for active employment ; prolonged vigils and intense application still farther contract his span, and make his time glide insensibly away. . . . It is enough that the age has already yielded instances of men pressing foremost in the lists of fame, and worthy of better times, schooled by continued adversity into an hatred of their kind, flying from thought to drunkenness, yielding to the united pressure of labour, penury, and sorrow, sinking unheeded, without one friend to drop a tear on their unattended obsequies, and indebted to charity for a grave among the dregs of mankind."

The title-page of the " Enquiry " was without an author's name ; but Goldsmith made no secret of his connection with the book. It was fairly received. The

Gentleman's published a long letter respecting it, and the two Reviews (the *Monthly* and the *Critical*) gave reports of its contents, both coloured, more or less, by a sense of the references which they detected in it to themselves. Smollett, in the *Critical*, was hurt that "a work undertaken from public spirit," such as his own, should be confused with "one supported for the sordid purposes of a bookseller" such as Griffiths; and the bookseller on his side did not omit, in the true spirit of vulgar reprisal, to salt his notice with unworthy innuendoes directed at his own not very satisfactory relations with Goldsmith. Such a course was to be expected in such a warfare; and it is idle now to grow virtuously indignant, because, read by the light of Goldsmith's later fame, these old injuries seem all the blacker. What most concerns us at present is that the "Enquiry" was Goldsmith's first original work, and that he revealed in it the dawning graces of a style, which, as yet occasionally elliptical and jerky, and disfigured here and there by Johnsonian constructions, nevertheless ran bright and clear. Acting upon his maxim that "to be dull and dronish, is an encroachment on the prerogative of a folio," he had, moreover, successfully avoided that "didactic stiffness of wisdom," which he declared to be the prevailing vice of the performances of his day. "The most diminutive son of fame, or of famine," he said, "has his *we* and his *us*, his *firstlys* and his *secondlys* as methodical, as if bound in cow-hide, and closed with clasps of brass." His own work could not be accused justly of this defect. But on the whole, and looking to the main purpose of his pages, it must be conceded that he made better use of his continental experiences in the descriptive passages of "The Traveller" than in the critical apothegms of "An Enquiry into the Present State of Polite Learning in Europe."

The "Enquiry," however, had one salutary effect: it attracted some of the more sagacious of the bookselling trade to the freshness and vivacity of the writer's manner. Towards the close of 1759 he is contributing both prose and verse to three periodicals, *The Bee*, *The Lady's Magazine*, and *The Busy Body*. The first two were published by J. Wilkie, at the Bible in St. Paul's Churchyard; the last, a paper in the old *Spectator* form — for which Goldsmith wrote, among other things, an excellent essay on the Clubs of London — by one Pottinger. But the fullest exhibition of his growing strength and variety is to be found in the eight, or rather the seven numbers, since the last is mainly borrowed, of *The Bee*, further described as "a select Collection of Essays on the most Interesting and Entertaining Subjects." The motto was—

> " Floriferis ut apes saltibus omnia libant
> Omnia nos itidem,"—

from Lucretius, and it was issued in threepenny parts, twelve forming "a handsome pocket volume," to which was to be prefixed the orthodox "emblematical frontispiece." Some of the contents were merely translations from Voltaire, upon whose "Memoirs," we know, Goldsmith had recently been working; some, such as "The History of Hypatia," the heroine of Charles Kingsley's novel, were historical and biographical; others again,—for example, "The Story of Alcander and Septimius," and "Sabinus and Olinda,"—were more

or less original. But the distinctive feature of the book
is the marked ability of its critical and social sketches.
The theatrical papers, with their neat contrast between
French and English actors, as regards what, in "The
Deserted Village," the author calls "gestic lore," their
excellent portrait of Mademoiselle Clairon, their shrewd
discerning of stage improprieties, and their just apprecia-
tion of "High Life below Stairs," are still well worth
reading. Not less excellent are the capital character
sketches, after the manner of Addison and Steele, of Jack
Spindle, with his "many friends," and "my Cousin
Hannah" in all the glories of her white *negligée*, her
wintry charms, and her youthful finery. In a paper
"On the Pride and Luxury of the Middling Class of
People," he anticipates certain of the later couplets of
his didactic poems ; in another, "On the Sagacity of
some Insects," he gives a foretaste of that delicate and
minute habit of observation which dictated not a few of
the happier pages of "The History of Animated Nature,"
while in an account of the Academies of Italy, he reverts
to the theme of the "Enquiry." Among the remaining
papers two chiefly deserve notice. One, "A City Night-
Piece," a title obviously suggested by Parnell, is tremulous
with that unfeigned compassion for the miseries of his
kind with which he had walked the London streets ; the
other, a semi-allegoric sketch in No. v., a little in the
Lucianic spirit of Fielding's "Journey from this World
to the Next," is interesting for its references to some of
his contemporaries. It is entitled "A Resverie," in
which the luminaries of literature are figured as passengers by a stage-coach, christened "The Fame

Machine." The coachman has just returned from his last
trip to the Temple of Fame, having carried as passengers
Addison, Swift, Pope, Steele, Congreve, and Colley
Cibber, and the journey has been accomplished with no
worse mishap than a black eye given by Colley to Mr.
Pope. (Had Fielding been of the party, as he should
have been, that black eye would certainly have been
repaid!) Among the next batch of candidates are Hill,
the quack author of "The Inspector," and the dramatist
Arthur Murphy, both of whom are declined by Jehu.
Hume, who is refused a seat for his theological essays,
obtains one for his history ; and Smollett, who fails with
his history, succeeds with his novels. Another intending
passenger is Johnson, and the page describing his proceedings is worth quoting for its ingenious tissue of
praise and blame :—

" This was a very grave personage, whom at some dis-
tance I took for one of the most reserved, and even
disagreeable figures I had seen ; but as he approached,
his appearance improved, and when I could distinguish
him thoroughly, I perceived, that, in spite of the severity
of his brow, he had one of the most good-natured
countenances that could be imagined. Upon coming to
open the stage door, he lifted a parcel of folios into the
seat before him, but our inquisitorial coachman at once
shoved them out again. 'What, not take in my dictionary!' exclaimed the other in a rage. 'Be patient,
sir,' (replyed the coachman) 'I have drove a coach, man
and boy, these two thousand years ; but I do not remember to have carried above one dictionary during the whole

time. That little book which I perceive peeping from
one of your pockets, may I presume to ask what it contains ? ' 'A mere trifle,' (replied the author) 'it is called
the Rambler.' 'The Rambler !' (says the coachman) 'I
beg, sir, you'll take your place ; I have heard our ladies
in the court of Apollo frequently mention it with rap-
ture ; and Clio, who happens to be a little grave, has been
heard to prefer it to the Spectator ; though others have
observed, that the reflections, by being refined, sometimes
become minute.' "

At this date (November, 1759) there seems to have
been no personal acquaintance between Johnson, whose
"Rasselas" had followed hard upon the "Enquiry," and
the still obscure essayist of Green Arbour Court. But
the friendship between the two was not now to be
long deferred, and may indeed have been hastened by
the foregoing tribute from the younger man.

There is one feature of Goldsmith's labours for Messrs.
Wilkie and Pottinger which deserves a final word.
Scattered through *The Bee* and *The Busy Body* are several
pieces of verse, which, if we except a translation
of part of a Latin prologue from Macrobius, included
in the first edition of the "Enquiry," constitute the
earliest of Goldsmith's published poetical works. Only
one of these, some not very remarkable quatrains on the
death of Wolfe, can be said to be original; the rest
are imitations. "The Logicians Refuted" is indeed so
close a copy of Swift as to have been included by Scott
among that writer's works ; the others, with one exception,
are variations from the French. They comprise two well-

known examples of the author's lighter manner. In "The Gift : To Iris, in Bow-Street, Covent Garden," he manages to marry something of Gallic vivacity to the numbers of Prior ; in the " Elegy on Mrs. Mary Blaize," borrowing a trick from the old song of M. de la Palisse, and an epigrammatic finish from Voltaire, he contrives to laugh anew at the many imitators of Gray. If they do no more, these trifles at least serve to show that the lightness of touch, which is one of his characteristics, had not been studied exclusively on English soil.

CHAPTER V.

THE visitors to Green Arbour Court were not always as illustrious as the Reverend Thomas Percy. One day, according to an informant from whom Prior collected some particulars respecting Goldsmith's residence at the top of Breakneck Steps, a caller was shown up to him with that absence of ceremony which was the hospitable rule of his house, and the door of the room was shortly afterwards locked with decision. Sounds of controversy succeeded. But, as both voices were heard in turn (*amant alterna Camœnæ!*), and the tumult gradually subsided, the apprehensions of the listeners also passed away. Late in the evening the door was unfastened, the stranger dispatched a messenger to a neighbouring tavern to order supper, and "the gentlemen who met so ungraciously at first, spent the remainder of the evening in great good humour." The explanation of this incident, which, in all probability, belongs to the last months of 1759, is that Goldsmith had been behindhand when Mr. Pottinger, or Mr. Wilkie of St. Paul's Churchyard, was clamouring for "copy" for the next number of *The Bee* or *The Busy Body*, and that the entertainment was the consideration offered for the unwonted course taken to obtain the required manuscript. It may also serve to throw some light on the short existences of those periodicals, by referring them to the uncertain inspiration or fastidious taste of the principal writer. " I could not suppress my lurking passion for applause," says George Primrose ; " but usually consumed that time in efforts after excellence which takes up but little room, when it should have been more advantageously employed in the diffusive productions of fruitful mediocrity. . . . Philautos, Philalethes, Philelutheros, and Philanthropos, all wrote better, because they wrote faster, than I."

But, in spite of these drawbacks, the literary quality manifested in the two periodicals above referred to, although they were powerless to catch the ear of the general reader, was still too unmistakeable to be neglected by those on the alert for fresh talent. Towards the end of 1759, two persons made their way to Green Arbour Court, both of whom were bent on securing Goldsmith's collaboration in new enterprises. One was Dr. Tobias Smollett, author of " Roderick Random" and " Peregrine Pickle," at this time fresh from imprisonment in the King's Bench, to which he had been subjected for his too frank criticism of Admiral Knowles ; the other was a pimple-faced and bustling little bookseller of St. Paul's Churchyard, John Newbery by name, whose ubiquitous energy his friend Dr. Johnson had playfully satirised in *The Idler* under the character of " Jack Whirler." Smollett, not, it may be imagined, less amiably disposed on account of the little compliment in the paper on the " Fame Machine " referred to in the last chapter, wished to obtain Goldsmith's services for a new magazine, *The*

British, which appeared on the 1st of January, 1760, with a flaming dedication to Mr. Pitt, and the opening chapters of the editor's new novel of "Sir Launcelot Greaves." For this latest recruit to the already crowded ranks of the monthlies, Goldsmith wrote some of the best of the papers afterwards reprinted among his "Essays." In the February and two subsequent numbers came that admirable "Reverie at the Boar's Head Tavern in Eastcheap," which rubs so much of the gilt off the good old times. In May followed an allegory in the popular taste : in June a comparison between two rival sirens at Vauxhall, Mrs. Vincent and Miss Brent, which is also a piece of close musical criticism. Three other contributions succeeded in July, one of which, "The History of Miss Stanton," it has been the custom to regard as a kind of early draught of the "Vicar of Wakefield." Goldsmith was so economical of his good things, and used them so often, that it is, of course, not impossible the "first rude germ" of his famous novel may lie in this "true though artless tale" of a seduction. Yet the "Vicar" would be little if it contained no more than is outlined in the character-less and rather absurd contribution to Smollett's magazine. Indeed, the conclusion is so "artless" as to justify a doubt whether the paper should really be attributed to Goldsmith's pen at all. At the end the seducer and the incensed parent exchange shots ; the latter "falls forward to the ground" and his daughter "falls lifeless upon the body. . . . Though Mr. Dawson [the villain of the piece] was before untouched with the infamy he had brought upon virtuous innocence," the story goes on to say, "yet he had not a heart of stone ; and bursting into anguish, flew to the lovely mourner, and offered that moment to repair his foul offences by matrimony. The old man, *who had only pretended to be dead*, now rising up, claimed the performance of his pr omise, and *the other had too much honour to refuse.* They were immediately conducted to church, where they were married, and now live exemplary instances of conjugal love and fidelity." Either Goldsmith is not guilty of this farrago of foolery and anticlimax (the italicised passages in which may be specially commended to notice) or it must once more be owned that truth is inconceivably stranger than fiction.

But although, in the opinion of the present writer, Miss Stanton's equivocal " history " is to be classed among the doubtful contributions of Goldsmith to *The British Magazine,* there are some other pieces concerning which there is no necessity to speak hesitatingly. Two of these, indeed, like the " Reverie at the Boar's Head," were afterwards included among the acknowledged " Essays " of 1765. One is an excellent homily on the " Distresses of the Poor," as exemplified in the cheerful philosophy of an humble optimist, who, battered almost out of shape by war and privations, still contrives to bless God that he enjoys good health, and knows of no enemy in the world save the French and the Justice of the Peace. The other, in which a shabby fellow, found lounging in St. James's Park, relates the "Adventures of a Strolling Player," has already been referred to in chapter iii., as probably reproducing some of the writer's own histrionic experiences. By October, 1760, however, the month in which it was published, Goldsmith was already well advanced in a continuous series of papers which were to prove of far greater importance than his occasional efforts for Smollett. A few days after the publication of the first number of *The British Magazine*, appeared the first number of another of Newbery's projects, the daily paper entitled *The Public Ledger*. For this also he had secured the services of Goldsmith, who was to write twice a week at the modest rate of a guinea per article. One of the earliest of his efforts was what would now be regarded as a heinous piece of partisanship, an adroit but unblushing puff of *The British Magazine*, and Smollett's novel therein. But before this appeared he had already established a hold upon the *Ledger's* readers. With a short letter in the number for January 24th, he had introduced to England a Chinese visitor— one Lien Chi Altangi. Five days later came another epistle from this personage to a merchant in Amsterdam, giving his impressions of London, its streets and its sign-boards, its gloom and its gutters. A third letter, addressed to a friend in China, laughed with assumed Oriental gravity at its men and women of fashion. Thus, without method, and almost by a natural growth, began the famous work afterwards known as "The Citizen of the World."

The "Chinese Letters," as they soon came to be called, progressed through 1760 with great regularity, and were completed, though rather more tardily, in the following year, under which date it will be most convenient to speak of them. For the moment, we may return to the chronicle of their writer's life. Besides his work for the *Ledger* and *The British Magazine*, he resumed his old connection with *The Lady's Magazine* in the new capacity of editor, and raised its circulation considerably.

He also contributed some serious biographies to *The Christian Magazine* of Dr. Dodd, who was afterwards executed for forgery. All this denotes varied activity and continuous occupation. His means at this time must have been sufficient, and, as a consequence, he moved, at the close of 1760, into better lodgings at No. 6, Wine Office Court, nearly opposite that ancient hostelry of the "Cheshire Cheese," still dear to the praisers of time past as a "murmurous haunt" of Johnson and his friends. Goldsmith occupied these lodgings for about two years; and it was here, according to the "Percy Memoir," that, on May 31, 1761, he received his first visit from Johnson, whom he had asked to supper. "One of the company then invited,"—this is the decorous circumlocution used for Percy by those who compiled the Memoir of 1801,— "being intimate with our great Lexicographer, was desired to call upon him and take him with him. As they went together, the former was much struck by the studied neatness of Johnson's dress: he had on a new suit of cloaths, a new wig nicely powdered, and everything about him so perfectly dissimilar from his usual habits and appearance, that his companion could not help inquiring the cause of this singular transformation. 'Why, sir,' said Johnson, 'I hear that Goldsmith, who is a very great sloven, justifies his disregard of cleanliness and decency, by quoting my practice, and I am desirous this night to show him a better example.'"

Boswell did not make Johnson's acquaintance until two years after this occurrence, and there is therefore no further account of this memorable entertainment. Beyond the publication in *The Lady's Magazine* of the

"Memoirs of Voltaire," nothing notable seems to have happened to Goldsmith in the remaining months of 1761. Probably he was at work for Newbery, for early in the following year, he issued a "History of Mecklenburgh," a concession to the anticipated interest in Queen Charlotte, and a pamphlet on the Cock Lane Ghost, which has been identified plausibly, but not conclusively, with one bearing the title of "The Mystery Revealed," put forth by Newbery's neighbour, Bristow. Cock Lane, it may be added, was close to Goldsmith's old residence in Green Arbour Court, so that in any case he would be in familiar neighbourhood. Then in May, 1762, in "two volumes of the usual *Spectator* size," that is, in *duodecimo*, and "Printed for the Author," who still preserved what was now the merest figment of anonymity, appeared the collected "Chinese Letters," under the title of "The Citizen of the World; or, Letters from a Chinese Philosopher, residing in London, to his Friends in the East." The phrase "Citizen of the World," was one Goldsmith had already used more than once, and it had the advantage of greater novelty than "Chinese Letters," a title, moreover, which had already been anticipated by the "Lettres Chinoises," published by the Marquis d'Argens. The completed issue was heralded by one of the author's most characteristic prefaces; and his prefaces, like his dedications, have always their distinctive touch. Speaking of the relation between his creation and himself, after recapitulating some of his efforts to preserve an Oriental local colouring (even to the item of occasional dulness), he says: "We are told in an old romance of a certain knight errant and his horse who contracted an intimate friendship. The horse most usually bore the knight, but, in cases of extraordinary dispatch, the knight returned the favour, and carried his horse. Thus in the intimacy between my author and me, he has usually given me a lift of his Eastern sublimity, and I have sometimes given him a return of my colloquial ease." Then, after a dream, in which he represents himself as wheeling his barrowful of " Chinese morality" on the cracking ice of " Fashion Fair," he continues, " I cannot help wishing that the pains taken in giving this correspondence an English dress, had been employed in contriving new political systems, or new plots for farces. I might then have taken my station in the world, either as a poet or a philosopher, and made one in those little societies where men club to raise each other's reputation. But at present I belong to no particular class. I resemble one of those solitary animals, that has been forced from its forest to gratify human curiosity. My earliest wish was to escape unheeded through life; but I have been set up for half-pence, to fret and scamper at the end of my chain. Tho' none are injured by my rage, I am naturally too savage to court any friends by fawning ; too obstinate to be taught new tricks ; and too improvident to mind what may happen : I am appeased, though not contented. Too indolent for intrigue, and too timid to push for favour, I am—But what signifies what am I." And thereupon he winds up with a Greek couplet very much to the same effect as that with which Señor Gil Blas of Santillane concludes the first conclusion of his delectable history.[1]

[1] In the later editions the following translation is added :
    " Fortune and Hope, adieu !—I see my port :
      Too long your dupe—be others now your sport."

In some of the advertisements of "The Citizen of the World" it was announced that the greater part of the work "was written by Dr. Goldsmith." This is a misconception, which arose from the fact that he had included among the epistles of Lien Chi Altangi a few of the anonymous contributions he had supplied to *The Bee* and other periodicals. Thus, "The City Night Piece" reappears as letter cxvii., and "The Distresses of a Common Soldier," from *The British Magazine*, as letter cxix. Haste and pressure may, in the first instance, have prompted these revivals ; but they were perfectly defensible, especially if we remember, as Goldsmith himself illustrates by a pleasant anecdote in the preface to a later volume, that the author who is preyed upon by others has certainly a prior right to prey upon himself. Omitting these, however, and omitting also those which are inspired by the scheme, and which deal chiefly with memories of Du Halde, Le Comte, and the other authorities on China consulted by Goldsmith, there remains a far larger amount of material than could be analyzed in these pages. The mind of the author, stored with the miscellaneous observations of thirty years, turns from one subject to another, with a freshness and a variety which delight us almost as much as they must have delighted the readers of his own day. Now he is poking admirable fun at that fashionable type, already the butt of Hogarth and Reynolds, the fine-art connoisseur, whom he exhibits writing enthusiastically from abroad to his noble father to tell him that a notable torso, hitherto thought to be "a Cleopatra bathing," has turned out to be "a Hercules spinning ; " now, in an account of a journey to Kentish

Town after the manner of modern voyagers, he ridicules
the pompous trivialities of travellers. Another paper
laughs at the folly of funeral elegies upon the great;
another at the absurdity of titles. More than one of the
Chinese philosopher's effusions are devoted to contemporary quacks, the Rocks and Wards, and so forth, who
engross the advertisement sheets of the day; others treat of
the love for monsters, of the trains of the ladies, of their
passion for paint and gaming. There is an essay on the
behaviour of the congregation at St. Paul's, to which it
would be easy to find a counterpart in Steele; there is
another on the bad taste of making a show out of the
tombs and monuments in Westminster Abbey, which
recalls Addison. Literature, of course, is not neglected.
Some of its humbler professors are hit off in the description of the Saturday Club at "The Broom near Islington";
other and graver utterances lament the decay of poetry,
the taste for obscene novels ("Tristram Shandy," to wit),
the folly of useless disquisitions among the learned, the
impossibility of success without means or intrigue. The
theatre also receives its full share of attention, as do the
coronation, the courts of justice, and the racecourse at
Newmarket. Mourning, mad dogs, the Marriage Act,
have each and all their turn, nor does Lien Chi Altangi
omit to touch upon such graver subjects as the horrors
of the penal laws and the low standard of public morality.

But what perhaps is a more interesting feature of the
Chinese philosopher's pages than even his ethical disquisitions, is the evidence they afford of the coming creator
of Tony Lumpkin and Dr. Primrose. In the admirable
portrait of the "Man in Black," with his "reluctant

goodness" and his Goldsmith family traits, there is a foretaste of some of the most charming characteristics of the vicar of Wakefield ; while in the picture of the pinched and tarnished little beau, with his mechanical chatter about the Countess of All-Night and the Duke of Piccadilly, set to the forlorn burden of "lend me half-a-crown," he adds a character-sketch, however lightly touched, to that immortal gallery which contains the finished full-lengths of Parson Adams and Squire Western, of Matthew Bramble and "my Uncle Toby." From the fact that he omitted the third of the "Beau Tibbs" series from the later "Essays" of 1765, it would seem that he thought the other two the better. It may be that they are more finely wrought ; but the account of the party at Vauxhall, with the delightful sparring of the beau's lady and the pawnbroker's widow, and the utter breakdown in the decorum of the latter, when, constrained by good-manners to listen to the faded vocalization of Mrs. Tibbs, she is baulked of her heart's desire, the diversion of the waterworks, is as fresh in its fidelity to human nature, and as eternally effective in its artistic oppositions of character, as any of the best efforts of the great masters of fiction.

One of the stories in " The Citizen of the World," that of " Prince Bonbennin and the White Mouse," has, rightly or wrongly, been connected with a ludicrous incident in Goldsmith's own career. Among his many hangers-on was a certain Pilkington,—the son, in fact, of Swift's Lætitia of that name,—who, on one occasion, called upon him with a cock-and-bull story about some white mice, which he, the said Pilkington, had (he alleged) been commissioned to obtain for a lady of quality, the Duchess of Manchester or Portland being mentioned. The mice had been secured; the ship that bore them lay in the river; and nothing—so ran Pilkington's romance— was wanting but a paltry two guineas to buy a cage, and enable the importer to make a decent appearance before his patroness. He accordingly applied to his old college-fellow, Goldsmith, who, not having the money, was, of course, easily cajoled into letting his necessitous friend pawn his watch. As might be expected, neither watch nor Pilkington was ever seen again, and Goldsmith was fain to console himself by composing a little apologue in his "Chinese Letters," in which white mice played a leading part. Another anecdote of this time is connected more with the study of manners which produced "The Citizen of the World" than with any particular utterance of Lien Chi Altangi. Once, when strolling in the gardens of White Conduit House at Islington, he came upon three ladies of his acquaintance, to whom he straightway proffered the entertainment of tea. The invitation was accepted, and the hospitality enjoyed, when, to Goldsmith's intense discomfiture, he suddenly discovered that he could not pay the bill. Luckily some friends arrived, who, after maliciously enjoying his embarrassment, at length released him from his quandary.

Upon the same day as "The Citizen of the World" was published, appeared the first instalment of another of those compilations for Newbery which Goldsmith, having tasted that dangerous delight of money advances for un-executed work, was tempted to undertake. This was a "Compendium of Biography" for young people, the opening volumes of which were based upon Plutarch's "Lives." It was intended to continue them indefinitely ; but seven volumes, the last of which was published in November, were all that appeared, "The British Plutarch" of Dilly proving a fatal rival. Before the fifth volume was finished Goldsmith fell ill, and it was completed by a bookseller's hack of the name of Collier. Whether Collier also did the sixth and seventh volumes does not appear. But Goldsmith's ill-health, caused mainly by the close application which had succeeded to the vagrant habits he had formed in early life, had now become confirmed, and he spent some part of this year at Tunbridge and Bath, then the approved resorts of invalids.[1] Early in the year one of Newbery's receipts shows that he had agreed to write, or had already written, a "Life of Richard Nash," the fantastic old Master of the Ceremonies at Bath. The book, which was published in October, is a gossipping volume of some two hundred and thirty pages, pleasantly interspersed with those anecdotes which Johnson thought essential to biography, and containing some interesting details upon the manners and customs of the old city, so dear to the pages of Anstey and Smollett. The price paid for it by Newbery, according to the receipt above mentioned, was fourteen guineas.

With one exception, nothing else of importance occurred to Goldsmith in 1762. This exception was the sale by him to a certain Benjamin Collins, printer, of Salisbury, for the sum of twenty guineas, of a third share

---

[1] "And once in seven years I'm seen
At Bath or Tunbridge to careen."

GREEN'S *Spleen.*

of a new book, in " 2 vols., 12mo.," either already written
or being written, and entitled " The Vicar of Wakefield."
The sale took place on the 28th October, and the circumstance, first disclosed by Mr. Charles Welsh in the
memoir of Newbery which he published in 1885, under
the title of " A Bookseller of the Last Century," throws a
new, if somewhat troubled, light upon the early history of
the " Vicar," as related by Goldsmith's biographers.
This question, however, will be more fitly discussed in a
future chapter.

CHAPTER VI.

WHETHER' the transaction referred to at the end of the last chapter took place at Salisbury, or whether Benjamin Collins made his investment in London, are points upon which there is no information. But it is not at all improbable that Goldsmith may have visited Salisbury in the autumn of 1762, and that the sale of the "Vicar" may have been the result of a sudden "lack of pence." Collins had business relations with Newbery. He was part-proprietor of that famous Fever Powder of Dr. James, upon which, in the sequel, Goldsmith so disastrously relied; and in Mr. Welsh's "Bookseller of the Last Century," he is also stated to have held shares in *The Public Ledger*, the idea of which he claimed to have originated. It is most likely therefore that, being known to Newbery, he was known to Goldsmith, and Goldsmith's appeal to Collins, when finding himself in the town in which Collins lived, would be a natural and intelligible step.

To pass however from conjecture to certainty, there is no doubt that, towards the end of 1762, Goldsmith, for the time at all events, transferred his residence from Wine Office Court to Islington, then a countrified suburb of

London. It was a place with which, apparently, he was already familiar, since he locates the Club of Authors in "The Citizen of the World" at the sign of The Broom, in that neighbourhood, and, in all likelihood, he had visited Newbery in his apartments at Canonbury House, of which nothing now remains but the dilapidated tower. He may even have lived in the tower itself previous to this date, for Francis Newbery, Newbery's son, affirmed that he lodged for some time in the upper story, "the situation so commonly devoted to poets." But that he came to Islington at the close of 1762 is clear from the Newbery papers, to which, when they wrote their respective lives of Goldsmith, Mr. John Murray permitted both Mr. Forster and Mr. Prior to have access. He had a room in a house kept by a Mrs. Elizabeth Fleming, who, like his Fleet Street landlady, was a friend or relative of Newbery. The bookseller, indeed, was paymaster in the business, deducting, with business-like regularity, the amount for Goldsmith's keep and incidental expenses, from the account current between the poet and himself. The "board and lodging" were at the rate of £50 per annum, and Goldsmith stayed at Mrs. Fleming's from Christmas, 1762, until June, 1764, or later, the only break being from December, 1763, to March in the following year, when he appears to have rented, but not occupied, his Islington hermitage.

It is curious in these days to study the chronicle of Goldsmith's frugal disbursements and hospitalities. Not many luxuries come within the range of Mrs. Fleming's recording pen. Once there is a modest "pint of Mountain" at a shilling, and twice "a bottle of port" at two shillings. A continually recurrent entry is the humble diet drink called " sassafras," more familiar perhaps as the " saloop," which, even at the beginning of this century, was still sold at street corners, prompting a characteristic page of Charles Lamb's " Praise of Chimney Sweepers," and surviving later in " Sketches by Boz." Pens and paper are naturally frequent items, and the " Newes man's " account, to wit, for *Public Ledgers, London Chronicles, Advertisers,* and the like, reaches the unprecedented sum of 16s. 10½d. On the other hand, " Mr. Baggott " and " Doctr. Reman " (Dr. Wm. Redmond, says Prior), who seem to have been occasionally entertained with dinner or tea, have " O. O. O.," against their names. Obviously, Goldsmith must either have shared his own meal with his guests, or Mrs. Fleming must have been a person whose generosities, however stealthy, did not blush to find themselves proclaimed in her bills. The only remaining items worth noting are the price of " a Post Letter," which, as now, was a penny, and that of " The Stage Coach to London," which was sixpence.

During most of the time over which these documents extend, Goldsmith must have been working for Newbery. The total amount paid by the bookseller from October, 1761, when Goldsmith purchased from him a set of Johnson's *Idler,* down to October 10, 1763, was £111 1s. 6d. At this date £63 had been earned by Goldsmith for " Copy of different kinds," leaving a balance against him of £48 1s. 6d., for which he gave a promissory note. The record of ascertained work for 1763 is very bare, so that the " copy " must chiefly have been prefaces, as for example, that to Brookes's " System of

Natural History," or revisions of Newbery's numberless
enterprises.   Only one work, the two *duodecimo* volumes
known as the " History of England, in a Series of Letters
from a Nobleman to his Son," can be identified as be-
longing to this time.   " His friend Cooke tells us," says
Mr. Forster, " not only that he had really written it in his
lodgings at Islington, but how and in what way he did
so."   Mr. Forster is here both right and wrong.   As the
" Letters of a Nobleman " were published in June, 1764,
it is most likely that they were written at Islington ; but
what Cooke actually says is, that they were written in a
country house on the Edgeware Road to which Goldsmith
does not seem to have gone until much later.   Cooke's
account of his composition of the letters may, however,
be accepted as accurate.   " His manner of compiling this
history was as follows :—he first read in a morning,
from Hume, Rapin, and sometimes Kennet, as much as
he designed for one letter, marking down the passages
referred to on a sheet of paper, with remarks.   He then
rode or walked out with a friend or two, who he con-
stantly had with him, returned to dinner, spent the day
generally convivially, without much drinking (which he
was never in the habit of), and when he went up to bed
took up his books and paper with him, where he generally
wrote the chapter, or the best part of it, before he went
to rest.   This latter exercise cost him very little trouble,
he said ; for having all his materials ready for him, he
wrote it with as much facility as a common letter."   The
book was a great success, in which the bookseller's artifice
of attributing it to a patrician pen no doubt played its
part.   For many years its easy, elegant pages were fathered

upon Chesterfield, Lyttelton, or Orrery, much to the amusement of the real author. But his friends knew well enough who the real author was, and both Percy and Johnson possessed presentation copies. Moreover when afterwards Goldsmith came to write his longer "History of England," for Davies of Russell Street, he transferred many passages bodily from the former compilation to the latter.

Among the friends who visited Goldsmith at Islington there is reason for believing that Hogarth is to be numbered. When he had made Goldsmith's acquaintance is not known ; but Goldsmith had referred to him in "The Enquiry," and may have been introduced to him by Johnson. The love of humour and character was strong in both ; but at this date they must have had an additional bond in their common dislike of Churchill. It is pleasant to think that the great pictorial satirist of his age may have sometimes been the strolling companion of his gentler brother with the pen. Years ago Mr. Graves, of Pall Mall, had in his possession a portrait, said to be by Hogarth, which passed under the name of "Goldsmith's Hostess," and "it involves," says Mr. Forster, "no great stretch of fancy to suppose it painted in the Islington lodgings, at some crisis of domestic pressure." As will be shown hereafter, there is no very trustworthy evidence that Mrs. Fleming was connected with any "domestic pressure ; " and the portrait, in all probability, had no graver origin than an act of kindness. In another picture, dating from this time, also attributed to Hogarth, which, when Mr. Forster wrote, belonged to a gentleman of Liverpool, Goldsmith is shown at work at a round table,

perhaps engaged upon one of the identical epistles ascribed
to Chesterfield. He is writing rapidly, or appears to be
writing rapidly, in a night cap and ruffles loose at the
wrist ; but, despite Mr. Forster's description, he seems
to be sitting for his likeness rather than to have been
sketched at work.

The first entry in Mrs. Fleming's account for 1764 is
an item of £1 17s. 6d. for the "Rent of the Room" for
the March quarter in that year, an entry which proves
conclusively that only by a figure of speech of the Dick
Swiveller type could Goldsmith's retreat be described as
"apartments." From the absence of other expenses, it
is clear that he was not in residence, and he does not
seem to have returned to Islington until the beginning of
April. In the interim he lived in London. One of his
occupations during this period must have been his weekly
attendances at the new club just formed upon a suggestion of Reynolds, whom somebody, for that reason,
christened its Romulus. Johnson, who had previously
belonged to a kindred gathering in Ivy Lane, now lapsed
or interrupted by the dispersal of its members, fell easily
into a proposition which accorded so thoroughly with his
gregarious habits, and other congenial spirits were
speedily collected. Edmund Burke and his father-in-law,
Dr. Nugent, Topham Beauclerk and Bennet Langton,
both of whom were scholars and fine gentlemen, Chamier,
afterwards an Under Secretary of State, John Hawkins, a
former member of the Ivy Lane Club, and Goldsmith
himself,—soon made up (with Reynolds and Johnson)
the nine members to which the association was at first
restricted. But a certain Samuel Dyer, another member

of the Ivy Lane Club, re-appearing unexpectedly from abroad, was allowed to join the ranks, and the number was ultimately extended to twelve. The place of meeting was the Turk's Head in Gerrard Street, Soho, "where," says Mr. Forster, "the chair being taken every Monday night at seven o'clock by a member in rotation, all were expected to attend and sup together." As time went on some further modifications were made in the rules; but at Gerrard Street the club continued to meet as long as Goldsmith lived, and it was not until nearly ten years after his death that, with the closing of the Turk's Head, it shifted its quarters. Such was the origin of the famous gathering, familiar in the pages of Boswell, and afterwards known—but not till many years afterwards—as the "Literary Club." A few of its first members were so illustrious that one can understand something of the astonishment with which solemn wiseacres like Hawkins beheld themselves associated with the still comparatively unknown recruit from Mrs. Fleming's at Islington. "As he wrote for the booksellers, we at the club," says he (but it would be probably more accurate to read "I"), "looked on him as a mere literary drudge, equal to the task of compiling and translating, but little capable of original, and, still less, of poetical composition." Pompous Mr. Hawkins may perhaps be forgiven for ignoring the fact that

> "the music of the moon
> Sleeps in the plain eggs of the nightingale,"—

especially as Goldsmith had hitherto published no verse with his name. But a more authoritative judge than the

Middlesex magistrate had already made deliverance upon the question. There was an eager young Scotchman of the name of James Boswell, who had decoyed Johnson into supping with him at The Mitre, and was already actively plying him with questions. Among other things he sought his opinion with regard to Goldsmith, whose apparently undeserved importance seems to have exercised him as much as it did Hawkins. On the literary side Johnson's answer was conclusive. " Dr. Goldsmith," he said, "is one of the first men we now have as an author." These words were uttered in June, 1763, when Goldsmith's reputation must have rested solely upon his labours as an essayist and compiler. For in that year he had not obtained distinction either as a poet, playwright, or novelist.

From April to June, 1764, Mrs. Fleming's accounts, as already observed, show that Goldsmith was again at Islington. He was probably employed for Newbery, but in what way is uncertain. One anecdote, however, is definitely connected with the forthcoming poem of "The Traveller," upon which he must have occupied his leisure. Prior tells it as it was told by Reynolds to Miss Mary Horneck, from whom, when Mrs. Gwyn, Prior again received it. "Either Reynolds," he says, "or a mutual friend who immediately communicated the story to him, calling at the lodgings of the Poet opened the door without ceremony, and discovered him, not in meditation, or in the throes of poetic birth, but in the boyish office of teaching a favourite dog to sit upright upon its haunches, or, as is commonly said, to beg. Occasionally he glanced his eye over his desk, and occasionally shook his finger

at his unwilling pupil in order to make him retain his
position, while on the page before him was written that
couplet, with the ink of the second line still wet, from
the description of Italy,

> ' By sports like these are all their cares beguiled,
> 　The sports of children satisfy the child.' "

Something of consonance between the verses and the
writer's occupation, seems at once to have struck the
visitor, and Goldsmith frankly admitted that the one had
suggested the other.

"The Traveller; or, a Prospect of Society, a Poem,"
was published on the 19th of December, 1764,[1] but the
title-page, as is often the case, bore the date of the
following year. It also announced that the book, published by Newbery as a thin eighteen-penny *quarto*, was
dedicated to the "Rev. Mr. Henry Goldsmith," and that it
was " by Oliver Goldsmith, M.B." The dedication,
which occupies nearly four pages, is extremely interesting.
The book, it says, is inscribed to Henry Goldsmith because some portions were formerly written to him from
Switzerland. "It will also throw a light upon many parts
of it," continues the writer, "when the reader understands

---

[1] There is no doubt that this is the practical *editio princeps*, as it
corresponds exactly with the description in the first advertisements.
But a well-known book-collector, Mr. Locker-Lampson, possesses a
copy, dated 1764, which would seem to indicate that Goldsmith had
not intended at first either to give prominence to his connection with
the poem, or to write a lengthy prefatory letter. No author's name
appears on the title-page of this unique copy, and the dedication is
confined to two lines : "This Poem is inscribed to the Rev. Henry
Goldsmith, M.A. By his most affectionate Brother Oliver Goldsmith."

that it is addressed to a man, who, despising Fame and Fortune, has retired early to Happiness and Obscurity with an income of forty pounds a year,"—such being the value of the curacy of Kilkenny West. Some of the passages that succeed are evidently dictated by the half-hopeful doubt of success which others besides Goldsmith have experienced. One of these,—the following,—was quietly dropped out of the subsequent editions, its anticipations, in the face of the favour with which the poem was received, being no longer appropriate. " But of all kinds of ambition, as things are now circumstanced, perhaps that which pursues poetical fame is the wildest. What from the encreased refinement of the times, from the diversity of judgments produced by opposing systems of criticism, and from the more prevalent divisions of opinion influenced by party, the strongest and happiest efforts can expect to please but in a very narrow circle. Though the poet were as sure of his aim as the imperial archer of antiquity, who boasted that he never missed the heart, yet would many of his shafts now fly at random, for the heart is too often in the wrong place." In the remainder of the dedication, the author renewed the assault which he had already made in the " Enquiry " upon the popularity of blank verse, and then proceeding to deplore the employment of poetry in the cause of faction, delivered himself of a thinly veiled attack upon the satires of Churchill—an attack which, seeing that Churchill had only been dead a few weeks, might well have been withheld. In his final words he defined the aim of his work : " I have endeavoured," he said, " to show, that there may be equal happiness in other states though differently governed from

our own ; that each state has a peculiar principle of happiness, and that this principle in each state, and in our own
in particular, may be carried to a mischievous excess."   In
another form this thought is to be found in the couplets
which, recalling one of his own precepts in " Rasselas,"
Johnson supplied at the end of " The Traveller " :—

> " How small, of all that human hearts endure,
>   That part which laws or kings can cause or cure.
>   Still to ourselves in every place consign'd,
>   Our own felicity we make or find."

The fact that Johnson contributed these lines and a
few others to the poem, seems to have favoured the suspicion that he had rendered considerable assistance to
the writer, and his dogmatic interpretation of a word in
the first line, while the real author was stammering and
hesitating for his meaning, served to strengthen this idea,
especially among persons of the Hawkins and Boswell
type.   But he distinctly told Boswell that he could only
remember to have written nine lines, four of which are
quoted above ; and (as Prior points out) his inexperience
of travel placed much of the rest beyond his ability.
Yet there is little doubt that he considerably influenced
the evolution of " The Traveller."   In the first place, it is
Johnson, not Pope or Dryden, who was Goldsmith's immediate model.   The measure of the poem is the
measure of " London " and " The Vanity of Human
Wishes," softened and chastened by a gentler touch and
a finer musical sense.   It was Johnson, too, Cooke tells
us, who persuaded Goldsmith to complete the fragment,
some two hundred lines, or rather less than half the

entire work, which he had so long kept by him. If conjecture is admissible in a matter of this kind, it would
seem most probable that what Goldsmith had already
written was the purely descriptive portions;[1] that Johnson,
so to speak, "moralized the song," and that, stimulated
by his critical encouragement, Goldsmith fitted these portions into the didactic framework which finally became
"The Traveller." But, however this may be, Johnson's
admiration of the result was genuine. Not only did he show,
by enthusiastic quotation long afterwards, that it lingered
in his memory, but he welcomed the poem himself in *The
Critical Review*, and congratulated the public upon it "as
on a production to which, since the death of Pope, it
would not be easy to find anything equal."

What shall be said now to that "philosophic Wanderer"
—as Johnson wished to christen him—who, in Wale's
vignette to the old *quarto* editions, surveys a conventional eighteenth-century landscape from an Alpine
solitude composed of stage rocks and a fir tree, and,
in Macaulay's words, "looks down on the boundless
prospect, reviews his long pilgrimage, recalls the varieties
of scenery, of climate, of government, of religion, of
national character, which he has observed, and comes
to the conclusion, just or unjust, that our happiness
depends little upon political institutions, and much on

[1] In these, it has been suggested, he had Addison's "Letter from
Italy" in mind, and a comparison of the two poems at once reveals
certain similarities. Moreover, that Goldsmith greatly admired the
"Letter from Italy" is proved by the fact that he included it both
in the "Poems for Young Ladies" and the "Beauties of English
Poesy."

the temper and regulation of our own minds?" We take
breath, and reply that we cannot regard his conclusion
as wholly just, or accept it without considerable reserva-
tion. We see difficulties in the proposition that one
government is as good as another, and we doubt whether
the happiness of the governed is really so independent
of the actions of the governing power. But what, to-day,
most interests us in "The Traveller," is its descriptive
and personal rather than its didactic side. If Goldsmith's precepts leave us languid, his charming topo-
graphy and his graceful memories, his tender retrospect,
and his genial sympathy with humanity still invite and
detain us. Most of us know the old couplets, but what
has Time taken from them of their ancient charm?—

> " Where'er I roam, whatever realms to see,
>   My heart untravell'd fondly turns to thee;
>   Still to my brother turns, with ceaseless pain,
>   And drags at each remove a lengthening chain.
>
>   Eternal blessings crown my earliest friend,
>   And round his dwelling guardian saints attend:
>   Bless'd be that spot, where cheerful guests retire
>   To pause from toil, and trim their ev'ning fire;
>   Bless'd that abode, where want and pain repair,
>   And every stranger finds a ready chair:
>   Bless'd be those feasts with simple plenty crown'd,
>   Where all the ruddy family around
>   Laugh at the jests or pranks that never fail,
>   Or sigh with pity at some mournful tale,
>   Or press the bashful stranger to his food,
>   And learn the luxury of doing good.
>
>   But me, not destin'd such delights to share,
>   My prime of life in wand'ring spent and care;

Impell'd, with steps unceasing, to pursue
Some fleeting good, that mocks me with the view;
That, like the circle bounding earth and skies,
Allures from far, yet, as I follow, flies;
My fortune leads to traverse realms alone,
And find no spot of all the world my own."

Equally well-remembered are the lines in which he records the humble musical performances by which he won his way through France :—

"To kinder skies, where gentler manners reign,
I turn; and France displays her bright domain.
Gay sprightly land of mirth and social ease,
Pleas'd with thyself, whom all the world can please,
How often have I led thy sportive choir,
With tuneless pipe, beside the murmuring Loire?
Where shading elms along the margin grew,
And, freshen'd from the wave the Zephyr flew;
And haply, though my harsh touch faltering still,
But mock'd all tune, and marr'd the dancer's skill;
Yet would the village praise my wondrous power,
And dance, forgetful of the noontide hour.
Alike all ages. Dames of ancient days
Have led their children through the mirthful maze,
And the gay grandsire, skill'd in gestic lore,
Has frisk'd beneath the burthen of threescore."

The description of Holland, "where the broad ocean leans against the land," and the lines on England, containing the familiar :—

"Pride in their port, defiance in their eye
I see the lords of human kind pass by,"

which his "illustrious friend" declaimed to Boswell in the Hebrides "with such energy that the tear started into his eye," might also find a place in a less-limited memoir than the present. Fortunately, however, there is no need to speak of a poem, which for three-quarters of a century has been an educational book, as if it were an undiscovered country. Nor can it add anything to a reputation so time-honoured to say that, when it first appeared, it obtained the suffrages of critics as various as Burke and Fox and Langton and Reynolds. The words of Johnson, spoken a century ago, are even truer now. Its merit is established; and individual praise or censure can neither augment nor diminish it.

The first edition, as we have said, appeared in December, 1764. A second, a third, and a fourth followed rapidly. There was a fifth in 1768, a sixth in 1770, and a ninth in 1774, the year of the author's death. He continued to revise it carefully up to the sixth edition, after which there do not seem to have been any further corrections. In one or two of the alterations, as in the cancelled passage in the dedication, is to be detected that reassurance as to recognition which prompts the removal of all traces of a less sanguine or prosperous past. In his first version he had spoken of his "ragged pride." In the second, this went the way of that indiscreet Latin quotation, which in the first edition of the "Enquiry" betrayed the pedestrian character of his continental experiences. But though the reception accorded to "The Traveller" was unmistakeable, even from the publisher's point of view, there is nothing to show with absolute certainty that its success brought any additional gain to its author. The original amount paid for "Copy of the Traveller, a Poem," as recorded in the Newbery MSS., is £21. There is no note of anything further; although, looking to the fact that the same sum occurs in some memoranda of a much later date than 1764, it is just possible (as Prior was inclined to believe) that the success of the book may have been followed by a supplementary fee.

CHAPTER VII.

ONE of the results of that sudden literary importance, which excited so much astonishment in the minds of the less discriminating of Goldsmith's contemporaries, was the inevitable revival of his earlier productions; and in June, 1765, Griffin of Fetter Lane put forth a three-shilling *duodecimo* of some two hundred and thirty pages under the title of "Essays: By Mr. Goldsmith." It bore the motto "*Collecta revirescunt*," and was embellished by a vignette from the hand of Bewick's friend and Stothard's rival, the engraver Isaac Taylor. In a characteristic preface Goldsmith gave his reasons for its publication. "Most of these essays," he said, "have been regularly reprinted twice or thrice a year, and conveyed to the public through the kennel of some engaging compilation. If there be a pride in multiplied editions, I have seen some of my labours sixteen times reprinted, and claimed by different parents as their own." And then he goes on, in a humourous anecdote, to vindicate his prior claim to any profit arising from his performances, finally winding up by a burlesque draft upon Posterity, which, as it is omitted in the second edition of 1766, may be reprinted here:

" Mr. Posterity. Sir, Nine hundred and ninety-nine years after sight hereof, pay the bearer, or order, a thousand pounds' worth of praise, free from all deductions whatsoever, it being a commodity that will then be very serviceable to him, and place it to the accompt of, &c."

Most of the papers contained in this volume have already been referred to in the preceding pages. Such are the " Reverie at the Boar's Head," the " Adventures of a Strolling Player," the " Distresses of a Common Soldier," and the " Beau Tibbs " sequence, only two of which it reproduces. There are others from *The Bee*, *The Busy Body*, and *The Lady's Magazine*. But the freshest contribution consists of a couple of poems, which figure at the end as Essays xxvi. and xxvii. One is " The Double Transformation," an obvious imitation of that easy manner of tale-telling, which Prior had learned from La Fontaine. Prior's method, however, is more accurately copied than his manner, for nothing is more foreign to Goldsmith's simple style than the profusion of purely allusive wit with which the author of "Alma" decorated his Muse. The other is an avowed imitation of Swift, entitled "A New Simile"; but it is hardly as good as "The Logicians Refuted," while indirectly it illustrates the inveteracy of that brogue which Goldsmith never lost, and, it is asserted, never cared to lose. No one but a confirmed Milesian would, we imagine, rhyme " stealing" and " failing." Elsewhere he scans "Sir Charles," " Sir Chorlus," after the manner of Captain Costigan; and more than once he pairs sounds like " sought " and "fault," a peculiarity only to be explained by a habit of mispronunciation.

One of the friends he had made by "The Traveller" was, like himself, an Irishman. This was Robert Nugent of Carlanstown, in Goldsmith's own county of Westmeath (not to be confounded with Dr. Nugent, Burke's father-in-law), who, two years later, was to be created Viscount Clare. Nugent was a poet in his way,—there are a number of his early verses in vol. ii. of Dodsley's "Collection;"— and his ode to William Pulteney was good enough to be quoted by Gibbon. His Essex seat became a frequent asylum to Goldsmith, who wrote for his friend a charming occasional poem, to which reference will be made hereafter. But for the present the most notable thing connected with Nugent is that he introduced Goldsmith to the notice of the Earl of Northumberland, then Lord-Lieutenant of Ireland, who, says Percy, being newly returned from that country in 1764, "invited our poet to an interview." It is supposed, though the "Percy Memoir" is here a little confusing, that this interview was the same as one of which Sir John Hawkins gives the following account in his "Life of Johnson": "Having one day," he says, "a call to wait on the late Duke, then Earl, of Northumberland, I found Goldsmith waiting for an audience in an outer room; I asked him what had brought him there: he told me, an invitation from his lordship. I made my business as short as I could, and, as a reason, mentioned that Doctor Goldsmith was waiting without. The Earl asked me if I was acquainted with him: I told him I was, adding what I thought likely to recommend him. I retired and staid in the outer room to take him home. Upon his coming out, I asked him the result of his conversation. 'His lordship,' says he, 'told me he had read my poem' meaning 'The Traveller,' 'and was much delighted with it; that he was going Lord-Lieutenant of Ireland, and that, hearing that I was a native of that country, he should be glad to do me any kindness.' 'And what did you answer,' asked I, 'to this gracious offer?' 'Why,' said he, 'I could say nothing but that I had a brother there, a clergyman, that stood in need of help: as for myself, I have no dependence on the promises of great men: I look to the booksellers for support; they are my best friends, and I am not inclined to forsake them for others." One can imagine what kind of effect this entirely unsophisticated proceeding would have upon the time-serving narrator of the anecdote; and indeed, his indignation blazes out in the comment with which he concludes his story. "Thus," he exclaims, "did this idiot in the affairs of the world trifle with his fortunes, and put back the hand that was held out to assist him! Other offers of a like kind he either rejected, or failed to improve, contenting himself with the patronage of one nobleman,[1] whose mansion afforded him the delight of a splendid table, and a retreat for a few days from the metropolis."

Few people, probably, will take Hawkins's view of the matter, or, at all events, they will find it difficult to conceive that Goldsmith, being Goldsmith, could have acted in any different way. His acquaintanceship with the Earl and Countess does not however seem to have suffered on this account. Possibly it was fostered by Percy, who, as their

---

[1] Nugent, as yet, was only " Mr." But Hawkins wrote his " Life of Johnson " many years after this date.

kinsman, should, one would think, have been the first to introduce the poet to his illustrious relatives. But the "Percy Memoir," as stated above, distinctly assigns this office to Nugent. Percy's "Reliques of Ancient Poetry," upon which he was then engaged, nevertheless, afforded opportunity for a further recognition of the poet by the Northumberlands. Out of many metrical discussions with Percy had grown a ballad in old style, to which Goldsmith gave the name of "Edwin and Angelina," although it was afterwards known as "The Hermit." The Countess of Northumberland admired it so much, that a few copies, now of the rarest, were struck off for her benefit, and it was afterwards included in "The Vicar of Wakefield." Goldsmith took immense pains with this poem. The privately printed version differs considerably from that in the "Vicar"; the text in the "Vicar" varies in the successive editions; and there are other variations in the volume of selections in which he afterwards included it. With its author, "Edwin and Angelina" was always a favourite. "As to my 'Hermit,' that poem," he told Cradock, "cannot be amended." And Hawkins only echoed contemporary opinion when he called it "one of the first poems of the lyric kind that our language has to boast of." We, who have heard so many clear-voiced singers since Goldsmith's time, can scarcely endorse that judgment, nor can we feel for it the enthusiasm which it excited when Percy's "Reliques" were opening new realms of freedom to those who had hitherto been prisoned in the trim parterres of Pope. At most we can allow it accomplishment and ease. But its sweetness has grown a little insipid, and its simplicity, to eyes unanointed with eighteenth-century sympathy, borders perilously upon the ludicrous.

In the same year in which "Edwin and Angelina" was printed, Goldsmith again attempted to earn a livelihood as a physician. This step, prompted by the uncertainty of his finances, is said to have been recommended by Reynolds, by Mrs. Montagu (to whom he had recently become known), and other friends. Evidence of his resumed profession speedily appeared in his tailor's account book, which, under the date of June, 1765, records the purchase of purple silk small clothes, and the orthodox "scarlet roquelaure buttoned to the chin" at four guineas and a half. These excesses must have been productive of others, for, in the short space of six months, three more suits are charged for, and this expenditure involves the complementary items of wig, cane, sword, and so forth. After these followed a man-servant. But all this lavish equipment seems to have failed in securing a practice. We hear, indeed, of one patient, whose moving story is told by Prior as he had received it from a lady [1] to whom Reynolds had related it : "He [Goldsmith] had been called in to a Mrs. Sidebotham, an acquaintance, labouring under illness, and having examined and considered the case, wrote his prescription. The quality or quantity of the medicine ordered, exciting the notice of the apothecary in attendance, he demurred to administer it to the patient ; an argument ensued, which had no effect in convincing either party of error, and some heat being produced by the contention, an appeal was at length made to the patient, to know by

[1] Mrs. Gwyn, *vide post*, p. 155.

whose opinion and practice she chose to abide. She, deeming the apothecary the better judge of the two from being longer in attendance, decided for him ; and Goldsmith quitted the house highly indignant, declaring to Sir Joshua he would leave off prescribing for friends. 'Do so, my dear Doctor,' replied Topham Beauclerk, when he heard the story, and afterwards jested with him on the subject; 'whenever you undertake to kill, let it be only your enemies.'"

The next noteworthy occurrence in Goldsmith's life is the publication, on the 27th of March, 1766, in "two Volumes in Twelves," of the novel of "The Vicar of Wakefield." The imprint was "Salisbury : Printed by B. Collins; For F. Newbery, in Pater-Noster-Row," by which latter it was advertised for sale, "Price 6s. bound, or 5s. sewed." There was no author's name on the title-page, but the "Advertisement" was signed "Oliver Goldsmith." The motto "*Sperate miseri, cavete felices,*" is to be found in Burton's "Anatomy," from which storehouse of quotation Goldsmith had probably borrowed it. Collins, the printer, it will be remembered, is the same person who, as related at the close of chapter v., had purchased a third share in the book for twenty guineas in October, 1762, more than three years before. That it was sold in this way is further confirmed by the fact that some years later, according to old accounts consulted by Mr. Welsh, it still belonged to Collins and two other shareholders, those shareholders being John Newbery's successors and Johnson's friend Strahan. This story of the sale is perfectly in accordance with eighteenth-century practice ; and, except that it is difficult to understand why the book remained so long unpublished, calls for no especial remark. And even the delay in publication can be explained by neglect on the author's part (not at all a fanciful supposition!) to put the finishing touches to work which had been already paid for. But the attraction of Mr. Welsh's discovery lies in its apparently destructive conflict with the time-honoured and picturesque narrative given (through Boswell) by Johnson, and by others for the most part deriving their data from him, of the original sale of the manuscript. It is as follows (vol. i. p. 225 of Boswell, 1st edn., 1791): "I [Johnson] received one morning a message from poor Goldsmith that he was in great distress, and, as it was not in his power to come to me, begging that I would come to him as soon as possible. I sent him a guinea, and promised to come to him directly. I accordingly went as soon as I was drest, and found that his landlady had arrested him for his rent, at which he was in a violent passion. I perceived that he had already changed my guinea, and had got a bottle of Madeira and a glass before him. I put the cork into the bottle, desired he would be calm, and began to talk to him of the means by which he might be extricated. He then told me that he had a novel ready for the press, which he produced to me. I looked into it, and saw its merit; told the landlady I should soon return; and having gone to a bookseller, sold it for sixty pounds. I brought Goldsmith the money, and he discharged his rent, not without rating his landlady in a high tone for having used him so ill."

Such is Boswell's report, taken, as he says, "authentically" from Johnson's "own exact narration." Elsewhere, recording a conversation at Sir Joshua Reynolds's, in April, 1778, he supplies some further particulars. "His 'Vicar of Wakefield,'" said Johnson, "I myself did not think would have had much success. It was written and sold to a bookseller before his 'Traveller'; but published after; so little expectation had the bookseller from it. Had it been sold after 'The Traveller,' he might have had twice as much money for it, though sixty guineas was no mean price." Here, it will be observed, Johnson says "guineas" instead of "pounds." But "pounds" and "guineas," as Croker points out in one of his notes, were then convertible terms. The same story, or rather a story having for its central features Goldsmith's need, Johnson's aid, and the consequent sale of a manuscript, is told with variations by other writers. Mrs. Piozzi, for example, in her "Anecdotes of Johnson," 1786, makes him leave her house to go to Goldsmith's assistance; but upon the question of the price, she only says that he brought back "some immediate relief." It is now known, however, that she did not make Johnson's acquaintance until January, 1765, and, looking to the express statement by Johnson that the "Vicar" was sold before the publication of "The Traveller" in December, 1764, is obviously at fault in one material point of her story. Hawkins, again, in his "Life of Johnson," 1787, gives a jumbled version, which places the occurrence at Canonbury House, makes the bookseller Newbery, and the amount forty pounds. Lastly Cumberland, writing his garrulous Memoirs in 1807, gives the incident as (he alleges) he had heard Dr. Johnson relate it "with infinite humour." In this account the publisher is Dodsley; the

price "ten pounds only"; and piquancy is added by an
unexpected detail. Goldsmith "was at his wit's-end how to
wipe off the score and keep a roof over his head, except
by closing with a very staggering proposal on her [his
landlady's] part, and taking his creditor to wife, whose
charms were very far from alluring, while her demands
were extremely urgent."

The foregoing accounts, that of Hawkins excepted, pro-
fess to be based upon Johnson's narrative of the facts.
From the only other actor in the drama, Goldsmith—if we
except a wholly incredible statement to Boswell that he had
received four hundred pounds for a novel, supposed to be
"The Vicar of Wakefield"—there is nothing except the
following passage in Cooke's reminiscences, which, probably because it was hopelessly at variance with the generally
accepted story, seems to have been entirely neglected by
Goldsmith's biographers. Cooke, doubtless, made some
mistakes ; but he is certainly entitled to be heard by the
side of Hawkins, Cumberland, and Mrs. Piozzi. "The
Doctor," he tells us, "soon after his acquaintance with
Newbery, for whom he held 'the pen of a ready writer,'
removed to lodgings in Wine Office Court, Fleet Street,
where he finished his 'Vicar of Wakefield,' and on which
his friend Newbery advanced him twenty guineas : 'A
sum,' says the Doctor, 'I was so little used to receive in
a lump, that I felt myself under the embarrassment of
Captain Brazen in the play,[1] "whether I should build a
privateer or a play-house with the money!"'" It will
be noted that, in more than one particular, this account

[1] *I.e.*, in the "Recruiting Officer," Act v., Sc. 3. Goldsmith
greatly admired Farquhar.

is confirmatory of the latest development of the story. It gives the value of a third share accurately; it describes it as an advance ; it makes the advancer Newbery, and, by implication, it places the occurrence in Wine Office Court, where Goldsmith lived to the end of 1762, in October of which year, either at Salisbury or London, Collins effected his purchase.

Unless some further discoveries are made, it is not likely that the above discrepancies can be finally adjusted. But as the latest editor of Boswell has thrown no light upon the subject, and the latest biographer of Johnson has handed it over to the biographers of Goldsmith, it is scarcely possible to quit the question without suggestion of some kind. The fact of Collins's purchase of a third share, resting as it does upon the evidence of his own account-books, which have been inspected by the present writer, is incontestable. The account of Johnson's sale of the manuscript, as Johnson, habitually "attentive to truth in the most minute particulars," originally gave it, is no doubt also essentially true, and its variations under other hands may be attributed in part to confused recollections of a confusing story. The mention of twenty guineas and forty pounds in two of the versions appears to indicate a confirmation of the sale by shares ; while the phrase " immediate relief" used by Mrs. Piozzi, and the "money for his relief" of Hawkins, suggest that Johnson may not have meant that he actually obtained the whole of the sixty pounds or guineas, but only that he had agreed upon that as the entire price, which he would have to do in order to establish the value of a share. If he only brought back part of the money, the case admits of plausible solution. Unless Boswell bungled terribly in his "exact narration," it is most improbable that the Collins sale preceded the Johnson sale. If it did, it involves, what is practically inadmissible, dishonesty on the part of Goldsmith or Johnson, in selling as a whole a book of which a part had already been disposed of. But if, on the other hand, the Johnson sale came before the Collins sale, the not unreasonable explanation would be that Johnson, called in, as he says, to Goldsmith's aid, went to Newbery or Strahan, settled upon the price of the manuscript, and procured for Goldsmith "immediate relief" in the shape of an advance for one or for two shares. The other share or shares would remain to be disposed of by the author, and so, either at Salisbury or London, the transfer to Collins would come about. The only objection to this supposition is, that it puts back the sale to 1762, instead of the usually accepted date of 1764. But 1764 has only been chosen because it is the year of the publication of "The Traveller." And it is noticeable that Boswell, who made Johnson's acquaintance in May, 1763, does not speak of the incident as if it had happened within his personal experience. On the other hand, in 1762, Goldsmith was at Wine Office Court, where, Cooke says, he finished the book. At Wine Office Court, we believe, the occurrence took place. It is more likely that Johnson, close at hand in Inner Temple Lane, would come to Wine Office Court than to Islington ; and it is not likely that Mrs. Fleming, the only evidence concerning whom, viz., her accounts, goes to show that she was not a particularly grasping personage, would arrest Goldsmith for bills which were usually paid by her friend

Mr. Newbery. In cases of this kind, it is necessary, as a first duty, to clear away structures that have been raised upon false data, and one of these is the traditional reputation, as an arbitrary person, of poor Mrs. Fleming of Islington. For, if the sale by Johnson took place in London, and not at Islington, Mrs. Fleming is not concerned in it.

But when Cooke says that the "Vicar" was finished at Wine Office Court, it is probable that he is not strictly accurate. What is most likely is, that when Goldsmith's pressure came, it was sufficiently finished to be sold. That it was written, or being written, in 1762, appears from the reference in chap. xix. to *The Auditor*, which began its career in June of that year, and from the mention in chap. ix. of the musical glasses then in vogue. But that it could not have been "ready for the press" is plain from the fact that the ballad of " Edwin and Angelina," privately printed in 1765 for the Countess of Northumberland, and first published in the novel, does not seem to have been in existence until about 1764. Percy says that it was composed before his own " Friar of Orders Gray," which came out in the " Reliques of English Poetry" in 1765, and Hawkins speaks of it in terms which imply that its composition belongs to some period subsequent to the establishment of "the Club" at the beginning of 1764. " Without informing any of us," says Hawkins, " he [Goldsmith] wrote and addressed to the Countess, afterwards Duchess of Northumberland, one of the first poems of the lyric kind that our language has to boast of." Although it is impossible to fix an exact date for the writing of " Edwin and Angelina," the

obvious inference is that it must have been written after
October 28, 1762, and consequently did not form part of
the book as sold to Collins.   Similarly, the " Elegy on a
Mad Dog," the scene of which lies at Islington, may have
been written there, and added to fill up.   In short, the
most reasonable supposition is that Goldsmith had
practically written his novel when he sold it to Collins
and Co., but that it required expansion to make up the
"two volumes, 12mo," which he had promised.   Probably
—as men do with work that has been paid for—he put
off making the necessary additions, and ultimately stopped
a gap with " Edwin and Angelina," which he had written
in the interim.   This, by the way, would supply a new
reason for the private printing of the ballad, namely, that
Goldsmith wanted to use it, or had already used it, in the
forthcoming "Vicar of Wakefield."   In any case, even when
the novel was published, it does not seem to have been
quite completed.   Criticism has pointed out that it
contains references showing that additions were intended
which were never made.   This is exactly what happens
when a work is sold before it is fully finished.   Moreover,
it has been noticed by a writer in the *Athenæum*, on in-
spection of the first issue, that, even with the assumed
additions, the printers had evidently hard work to make
up the required two volumes.   This, and the difficulty of
getting the author to supply the requisite " copy," may
indeed be the true solution of that long delay to publish,
which has surprised so many of Goldsmith's biographers.

Of the " Vicar " itself it is happily not necessary to give
any detailed account, still less to illustrate its beauties by
what Mr. Lowell has somewhere called the Bœotian

method of extract. Dr. Primrose and his wife, Olivia and Sophia, Moses with his white stockings and black ribbon, Mr. Burchell and his immortal " Fudge," My Lady Blarney and Miss Carolina Wilhelmina Amelia Skeggs—have all become household words. The family picture that could not be got into the house when it was painted ; the colt that was sold for a gross of green spectacles ; the patter about Sanchoniathon, Manetho, Berosus, and Ocellus Lucanus, with the other humours of Mr. Ephraim Jenkinson—these are part of our stock speech and current illustration. Whether the book is still much read it would be hard to say, for when a work has, so to speak, entered into the blood of a literature, it is often more recollected and transmitted by oral tradition than actually studied. But in spite of the inconsistencies of the plot, and the incoherencies of the story, it remains, and will continue to be, one of the first of our English classics. Its sweet humanity, its simplicity, its wisdom and its common-sense, its happy mingling of character and Christianity, will keep it sweet long after more ambitious, and in many respects abler, works have found their level with the great democracy of the forgotten.

It is the property of a masterpiece to gather about it a literature of illustration and interpretation, especially when, as in the present case, its origin is unusually obscure. With the bulk of this it would be impossible to deal here. But a recent speculation respecting the reasons for the choice of Wakefield as the locality of the tale (at all events at the outset), deserves a few sentences. Joseph Cradock, one of Goldsmith's later friends, had a story that the " Vicar " was written to defray the expenses

of a visit to Wakefield. How irreconcilable this is with
the other accounts is self-evident. But it is not impossible
that an actual tour in Yorkshire may have suggested some
of the names and incidents. This idea has been worked
out with great ingenuity by Mr. Edward Ford, of Enfield,
in an article contributed by him in May, 1883, to *The
National Review.* Starting from Wakefield, he identifies
the "small cure" seventy miles off, to which Dr. Primrose
moves in chap. iii., vol. i., with Kirkby Moorside in the
North Riding. This point established, Welbridge Fair,
where Moses sells the colt (chap. xii. and chap. vi., vol.
ii.), easily becomes Welburn ; Thornhill Castle, a few
miles further, stands for Helmsley ; "the wells" (chap.
xviii.) for Harrogate, and "the races" (*ibid*) for Don-
caster. The "rapid stream" in chap. iii., where Sophia
was nearly drowned, he conjectures to have been near
the confluence of the Swale and Ouse at Boroughbridge,
"within thirty miles" (p. 21) of Kirkby Moorside ; and
the county gaol in chap. v., vol. ii., he places "eleven
miles off" (p. 86) at Pickering. But for the further
details of this attractive if inconclusive inquiry, as well
as the conjectural identification of Sir William Thornhill,
with the equally eccentric Sir George Savile, and
of the travelling limner of chap. xvi., vol. i., with
Romney the artist, the reader is referred to the article
itself.

The first edition of the "Vicar," it will be remembered, was published on March 12, 1766. A second
edition, containing some minor modifications, one of the
most important of which was the reiteration, with great
effect, of Mr. Burchell's famous comment, followed in

May, and a third in August. In the same year there
were also two unauthorized reprints of the first edition,
one of which was published at Dublin, the other in
London. After this there seems to have been a lull in
the demand, for the fourth edition is dated 1770; and,
according to Collins's books, started with a loss. The
profits of this seem to have been so doubtful that, before
the fifth edition appeared, Collins sold his third share to
one of his colleagues for five guineas. The fifth edition,
which did not actually appear until April, 1774, is dated
1773. This would indicate that the previous issue was not
exhausted until early in the following year. The sixth
edition is dated 1779. Thus, assuming the fifth to have
been, like the fourth edition, limited to one thousand
copies, it took nearly nine years to sell two thousand
copies. No rival of any importance was in the field,
until, in 1778, Miss Burney published her " Evelina ; "
and the languor of the sale must be attributed to some
temporary suspension of public interest in the " Vicar."
Meanwhile, translations into French and German, to be
followed in due time by translations into almost every
European language, were laying the foundation of its cosmopolitan reputation, and its modern admirers still take
pleasure in recollecting that among the most famous of
their predecessors was Goethe. "It is not to be described,"
he wrote to Zelter in 1830, "the effect which Goldsmith's
'Vicar' had upon me just at the critical moment of
mental development. That lofty and benevolent irony,
that fair and indulgent view of all infirmities and faults,
that meekness under all calamities, that equanimity under
all changes and chances, and the whole train of kindred

virtues, whatever names they bear, proved my best education ; and in the end, these are the thoughts and feelings which have reclaimed us from all the errors of life."

CHAPTER VIII.

GOLDSMITH'S biographers have laid stress upon the fact that there is no record of any payment to him for the "Vicar of Wakefield," subsequent to that original sixty pounds, or guineas, whereof mention was made in the foregoing chapter; and they have not failed to remark, with a certain air of righteous indignation, that, on May 24, 1766, close upon the publication of the second edition, a bill drawn by him upon John Newbery for fifteen guineas was returned dishonoured. Some indignation would be intelligible, and perhaps justifiable, had the book been a pecuniary success, which, of course, was their assumption, an assumption based upon the rapid appearance of three editions. But, if Collins's accounts are to be relied upon, and the chief objection to them is their contradiction of accepted traditions, the "Vicar," in spite of those three editions (of how many copies we are ignorant), was not paying its proprietors—in other words, they had not yet recovered the £60 they had laid out upon the manuscript. No other interpretation can be placed upon the statement of Mr. Welsh, who says, "The fourth edition [of 1770] started with a loss." If so, no ground existed for any generosity from the proprietors to the author. On the other hand, "The Traveller" was a success. It had reached a fourth edition in August, 1765, and in a memorandum by Goldsmith printed by Prior, and dated June 7, 1766, there is an item of £21 for "The Traveller." It is scarcely possible that this can refer to the first payment made as far back as 1764, and it may therefore be assumed, not unreasonably, that it was an additional payment arising out of the success of the poem. If this be the case, the circumstances as regards the two books become perfectly logical, and neither surprise nor indignation is called for. The fourth edition of "The Vicar" started with a loss, and there were no profits for anybody ; the fourth edition of "The Traveller" had paid its expenses with a fair surplus, and there was a bonus of twenty guineas for the author.

But a dubious twenty-guinea bonus upon the sale of a popular poem is scarcely opulence, and Goldsmith was still obliged to depend upon the old "book-building." Between the appearance of the second and third editions of the "Vicar," there was issued by the "Vicar's" publisher, Francis Newbery, a translation of a "History of Philosophy and Philosophers," by M. Formey of Berlin, whose "Philosophical Miscellanies" Goldsmith had reviewed for Smollett in *The Critical Review*. For this, in pursuance of some occult arrangement between the Newberys, John Newbery paid—the sum being £20. Later in the year Goldsmith prepared for Payne of Paternoster Row, but without his name as editor, a selection of "Poems for Young Ladies," the "Moral" department of which led off with his own "Edwin and Angelina," a circumstance which lends a certain piquancy to the artless statement in the preface that "every poem in the following collection would singly have procured an author great reputation." Following hard upon the publication of this in December, comes the record of a " short English Grammar " for Newbery ; and then was prepared for Griffin " The Beauties of English Poesy," in two volumes, for which selection, with the addition of his name on the title-page, he was paid £50, or only £10 less than the sum he obtained for the " Vicar," an original work. His " original work " in this was confined to a preface, and brief introductory notes. But the success of this otherwise excellent anthology was prejudiced considerably by the presence in it of two of Prior's most hazardous pieces, the " Ladle " and " Hans Carvel," an intrusion all the more unwarrantable, because Prior's somewhat meagre individuality was already sufficiently represented by his poem of " Alma."

Not many months after the publication of the " Beauties," and prompted, it may be, by the reappearance of " Edwin and Angelina " in the " Poems for Young Ladies," Kenrick, Goldsmith's successor on *The Monthly Review*, and his persistent assailant, took occasion to bring against him a charge of gross plagiarism. A letter signed " Detector " appeared in the *St. James's Chronicle* in which he was accused of taking " The Hermit " (" Edwin and Angelina ") direct from Percy's " Friar of Orders Gray," with this difference only, that he had substituted " languid smoothness " and " tedious paraphrase " for the " natural simplicity and tenderness of the original." Several of the stanzas in the " Friar " are the beautiful snatches sung by Ophelia in her insanity, and Goldsmith might well have been absolved from improving upon them. But to the general charge of theft he replied conclusively in a letter to the *Chronicle* dated July, of which the following is the material portion : "Another Correspondent of yours accuses me of having taken a Ballad, I published some Time ago, from one by the ingenious Mr. Percy. I do not think there is any great Resemblance between the two Pieces in Question. If there be any, his Ballad is taken from mine. I read it to Mr. Percy some Years ago, and he (as we both considered these Things as Trifles at best) told me, with his usual Good Humour, the next Time I saw him, that he had taken my Plan to form the fragments of Shakespeare into a Ballad of his own. He then read me his little Cento, if I may so call it, and I highly approved it. Such petty Anecdotes as these are scarce worth printing, and were it not for the busy Disposition of some of your Correspondents, the Publick should never have known that he owes me the Hint of his Ballad, or that I am obliged to his Friendship and Learning for Communications of a much more important Nature." The reply is perfect in tone, and shows once more how unfailing was Goldsmith's skill when he took pen in hand. Percy, it may be added, confirmed this story, with but little variation, in a note which he appended to the "Friar of Orders Gray" in the 1775 edition of the "Reliques," and also in the "Memoir" of Goldsmith, prefixed to the "Miscellaneous Works" of 1801.

About the middle of 1767 Goldsmith seems to have again taken up his residence at Islington, and this time

it is definitely asserted that he lived in Canonbury House.
The old tower of Queen Elizabeth's hunting lodge was a
favourite summer resort of literary men, publishers, and
printers, and, as already stated, John Newbery himself,
who died in December of this year, was one of its most
frequent inmates. Indeed, some last business instructions
drawn up by him in November are dated " Canbury
House," and the notice of his death in *The Public
Advertiser* affirms that it actually occurred there. But
whether Goldsmith now occupied that " upper story
so commonly devoted to poets," or tenanted, either on
his own account, or as Newbery's substitute, the old
oak-panelled room on the first floor, long shown to visitors
as his, history sayeth not with any certainty. That he
attended, and occasionally presided at a club, largely
recruited from the lettered and quasi-lettered occupants
of Canonbury Tower, which was held at the Crown Tavern
in the Islington Lower Road, may be more safely assumed.
When in London, he occupied new quarters in the Temple, to which he had moved from his old home in Fleet
Street. These were in Garden Court, an address that
figures at the head of one of his letters to Colman, dated
July the 19th, and hence, in all probability, he penned
his letter to the *Chronicle.* According to Prior his
apartments were on the library staircase, and he shared
them with one Jeffs, butler to the Society. Consequently
there is no record of his residence in the books. Nor is
there any record of the somewhat superior lodging in
King's Bench Walks to which he removed a little later,
where he was again, apparently, the tenant of a private
owner. Neither of these retreats was of imposing cha-

racter, and Goldsmith's ready susceptibility took alarm when he saw Johnson blinking about, in his short-sighted way, at his friend's environment. " I shall soon be in better chambers than these," he said, apologetically. But his sturdy old mentor was down upon him at once with a " Nay, Sir, never mind that : *Nil te quæsiveris extra.*"

To another of his Temple visitors Goldsmith behaved with greater dignity. Towards the close of this same year of 1767 an attempt was made to enlist his pen in the service of that " party," to which, in the " dedication " of " The Traveller," he had referred as one of the enemies of his art. The North Administration, harassed by Wilkes, and goaded by the far more terrible " Junius," was casting about helplessly for literary champions, and overtures were accordingly made to Goldsmith by Sandwich's chaplain, Parson Scott, known to the contemporary caricaturist as " Twitcher's Advocate," a title he had earned by his support of his patron under the *nom de guerre* of *Anti-Sejanus.* Scott had already reaped the benefit of his "venal pen" by presentation to the living of Simonburn, in Northumberland, and appointment as Chaplain of Greenwich Hospital. The sequel of his visit to Goldsmith may be told in his own words : " I found him," said Dr. Scott to Basil Montagu, " in a miserable set of chambers in the Temple. I told him my authority; I told him that I was empowered to pay most liberally for his exertions ; and, would you believe it ! he was so absurd as to say, ' I can earn as much as will supply my wants without writing for any party. The assistance you offer is, therefore, unnecessary to me,' and so I left him," added Dr. Scott, " in his garret." The

contempt of the prosperous timeserver was to be anticipated, though Goldsmith's admirers will doubtless take a
different view of the matter.

But when Goldsmith told Lord North's emissary that
he was earning enough for his wants, it is to be feared
that the statement, like his earlier announcement to
Beatty of his prosperity as a physician in Southwark, was
a palpable exaggeration. Of lucrative work during 1767
there is scant indication. What he did for his old employer, Newbery, amounted to little ; and Newbery, it has
been shown, was ill or dying in the latter months of this
year. Yet a turn for the better was coming in Goldsmith's life, and during part of 1766 and 1767 he had
been engaged in a new enterprise, of which an account
will presently be given. In addition, about this time, a
somewhat more prosperous way of compilation was
opened by a proposal of the bookseller, Thomas Davies,
whose " very pretty wife " is celebrated in the verse of
Churchill. Davies had been shrewd enough to observe
that the " Letters from a Nobleman to his Son " of two
years before, still freely given to literary lords like
Chesterfield and Orrery, had lost none of their real
popularity or their fictitious prestige, and he hit upon
the happy idea of proposing to Goldsmith to write a
Roman History upon the same pattern. The honorarium
was to be two hundred and fifty guineas. There were
to be two volumes, to be finished in two years or less.
As the book was published in May, 1769, it must be
assumed that it had, or should have, begun to employ
Goldsmith actively in the later months of 1767.

There is little record of his other occupations. Doubtless, when in London, he was assiduous in his attendance at the Turk's Head, in Gerrard Street, on the Mondays when the club held its sittings. But he was probably more at home in resorts like the Crown, in the Islington Lower Road, where the company was less pretentious. One of these " free and easys," described by Mr. Forster from the manuscript notes of a certain William Ballantyne, lent to him by Mr. Bolton Corney, went by the name of the "Wednesday Club," and was held at the Globe Tavern, in Fleet Street. Among its frequenters were several of Goldsmith's countrymen—Glover, a doctor and actor, who afterwards wrote "Anecdotes of the late Dr. Goldsmith," for *The Annual Register* [1] ; Thompson, who edited Andrew Marvel ; and Hugh Kelly, a staymaker turned rhymester, who was imitating Churchill's "Rosciad" in a poem called " Thespis," and was shortly to become the pillar of sentimental comedy. Of the other members chronicled in Ballantyne's notes, the most memorable was a Mr. Gordon, a huge man, whom, to use Falstaff's words, " sighing and grief had blown up like a bladder," and who used to delight Goldsmith by singing a thoroughly appropriate song, called " Nottingham Ale." But it was noted, even at this time, that the old fits of silence and depression, which his relatives had remarked in his childhood, still haunted him. " He has often," says Glover, "left a party of convivial friends abruptly in the evening, in order to go home and brood over his misfortunes." Washington Irving's more charitable explanation is, that

[1] These, with additions, and some variations, were republished in the eighth edition of the " Retaliation," 1776, and in the " Poems and Plays," Dublin, 1777.

he went home to note down some good thing for his forthcoming comedy. But the hopes and fears connected with that enterprise were of themselves sufficient to cause depression, and to the story of those hopes and fears we now come.

Goldsmith had always been a fervent lover of the stage. As already stated, there are traditions that he had composed a tragedy, which he had submitted in manuscript to Richardson ; and in the " Enquiry," *The Bee,* " The Citizen of the World," and even in the " Vicar," he had frequently expressed his opinions upon matters theatrical, certainly with the knowledge, if not of a dramatist, at least of a shrewd and common-sense critic. At this date what, in addition to pantomime and spectacle, found most favour in England, was " genteel " or " sentimental comedy." This was the English equivalent for the *comédie sérieuse* or *larmoyante,* which, initiated in France by La Chaussée, had recently been most happily exemplified in that country by Sedaine's *Philosophe sans le savoir.* According to Diderot, this school had for its object not so much the satire of vice as the glorification of virtue—by virtue being meant more particularly the virtues of private and domestic life. Steele, at the beginning of the century, had attempted something of the kind in "The Funeral " and " The Lying Lover "; but the new French school, whose influence was now being felt on this side the Channel, had arisen long after he had ceased his labours as a dramatist. Goldsmith's views, it need scarcely be said, were entirely opposed to the prevailing fashion of comedy. He was, he tells us, strongly prepossessed in favour of the authors of the last age. Nature and humour, he contended, in whatever walks of life they were most conspicuous, should be the chief ends of the playwright, and the delineation of character his principal duty. By reason of the ultra-refinement and insipid unreality of the new manner, these things, in his opinion, were in a fair way to disappear from the stage altogether; and when, at the beginning of 1766, the success of "The Clandestine Marriage," which Colman and Garrick had adapted from Hogarth's most famous picture-drama, seemed to promise some chance of a re-action in the public taste, he straightway set to work upon a comedy on the elder English model. He appears to have wrought at it during 1766, in the intervals of his other literary work, and he had completed it early in 1767, when it was submitted to some of his friends, who approved it. Johnson undertook to write a prologue, and thereupon began the indispensable and traditionally wearisome negotiations for getting it placed upon the boards.

At this time Garrick was manager of Drury Lane. To Garrick, however, Goldsmith had not intended to apply. He knew that he had offended the all-powerful actor by certain passages still on record in the "Enquiry," and Garrick had shown his sense of this by refusing his vote when Goldsmith was a candidate for the secretary-ship of the Royal Society. Unhappily, owing to the death of its manager Rich, the affairs of the rival theatre of Covent Garden were in temporary confusion. Goldsmith had therefore no choice but to address himself to Garrick, and Reynolds arranged a meeting between them

at his house.   As may be anticipated, it was not entirely
satisfactory.   Goldsmith was sensitive and consequential ;
Garrick courteous, but cautious.   Nevertheless, there was
an indefinite understanding that the play should be acted.
The manager seems subsequently to have blown hot and
cold according to his wont.   In reality, he did not like
the piece, and he privately told Reynolds and Johnson
that he thought it would not succeed.   To the author
he was not equally frank, and thus misunderstandings
multiplied.   Meanwhile the theatrical season slipped
away, and Goldsmith, who had counted upon the
pecuniary profits of his work, grew impatient.   Finally
he asked for an advance upon a note of the younger
Newbery.   This was readily granted ; but the boon was
followed up by suggestions for alterations and omissions in
the play—alterations and omissions which, it is unnecessary to say, were anything but palatable to the
author.   Arbitration was next spoken of, and, in this
connection, William Whitehead, a man of very inferior
calibre, whom Garrick occasionally employed as his
reader, was named.   Thereupon, says Mr. Forster, "a
dispute of so much vehemence and anger ensued, that the
services of Burke as well as Reynolds were needed to
moderate the disputants."

But a sudden change in the state of affairs at the rival
house, fortunately opened the way to a solution of these
protracted differences.   Colman, by a sequence of circumstances which do not belong to these pages, became
one of the patentees of Covent Garden ; and Goldsmith
seized the opportunity for offering him his comedy.   He
promptly received an encouraging reply.   Forthwith he

wrote to Garrick stating what he had done ; and in return was gratified with one of those formally cordial responses in which the actor was an adept. But he had not yet reached the end of his troubles. It was in July, 1767, that he wrote to Colman, and his comedy could not be produced until Christmas. In the interval further complications arose. Garrick, already in hot competition with Covent Garden, was, naturally, not very favourably disposed to its newest dramatic writer ; and he accordingly, in opposition to Goldsmith's comedy, of which we may now speak by its name of " The Good Natur'd Man," brought forward Hugh Kelly with a characterless sentimental drama called " False Delicacy." Before the end of the year the " whirligig of time " had reconciled him to Colman, and one result of this was, that the latter, whose interest in Goldsmith's piece had meanwhile somewhat cooled, consented tacitly to keep back " The Good Natur'd Man " until " False Delicacy " had made its appearance. So it befell that, in January, 1768, when " The Good Natur'd Man " was going slowly through its last rehearsals, " False Delicacy " came out at Drury Lane with all the advantages of Garrick's consummate generalship. A few days later " The Good Natur'd Man " was played for the first time at Covent Garden. Johnson's prologue turned out to be rather dispiriting ; and Powell, Garrick's handsome young rival, was, as the hero, cold and unsympathetic. On the other hand, Shuter, an excellent actor, proved inimitable in the part of Croaker, a character planned upon the " Suspirius " of *The Rambler*, while Woodward was almost equally good as the charlatan, Lofty. The success of the piece, however, was only qualified, and one scene of "low" humour, in which some bailiffs were introduced, gave so much offence, that it was withdrawn after the first representation.

Goldsmith, who, as his tailor's bills testify, had attended the first night in a magnificent suit of "Tyrian bloom, satin grain, and garter blue silk breeches," and whose hopes and fears had risen and fallen many times during the performance, was bitterly disappointed. Nevertheless, after hurriedly thanking Shuter, he went away to the club in Gerrard Street, laughed loudly, made believe to sup, and ultimately sang his own particular song. Years afterwards, however, the truth leaked out. Coming back one day from dining at the chaplain's table at St. James's, Dr. Johnson told Mrs. Thrale that Goldsmith had been there giving "a very comical and unnecessarily exact recital of his own feelings when his play was hissed." He had told "the company how he went indeed to the Literary Club at night, and chatted gaily among his friends as if nothing had happened amiss ; that to impress them more strongly with his magnanimity, he even sung his favourite song about an old woman tossed in a blanket seventeen times as high as the moon, 'but all this time I was suffering horrid tortures (said he), and verily believe that if I had put a bit in my mouth it would have strangled me on the spot, I was so excessively ill ; but I made more noise than usual to cover all that, and so they never perceived my not eating, nor, I believe, imaged to themselves the anguish of my heart : but when all were gone except Johnson here, I burst out a-crying, and even swore by —— that I would never write again.' 'All which, Doctor (says Mr. Johnson, amazed at his odd frankness), I thought had been a secret between you and me ; and I am sure I would not have said anything about it for the world.' " " No man," added Johnson, commenting upon his own story, " should be expected to sympathize with the sorrows of vanity." And then he went on to make some further remarks upon the subject which show once more how much easier are precepts than practice.

" The Good Natur'd Man " was played for ten consecutive nights, being commanded on the fifth by their Majesties. The third, the sixth, and the ninth nights were appropriated to the author. By these he made about £400, to which the sale of the play in book form with the suppressed bailiff scene restored added another £100. It seems clear, notwithstanding, that the play was not such a success as it deserved to be ; and that much was done to protract its brief life by the author's friends. The taste for sentimental comedy, in fact, was still too strong to be overcome. Yet, as Davies points out, and Davies as a former actor is an authority, " The Good Natur'd Man " contains " two characters absolutely unknown before to the English stage ; a man [Lofty] who boasts an intimacy with persons of high rank whom he never saw, and another, who is almost always lamenting misfortunes which he never knew. Croaker [he asserts] is as strongly designed, and as highly finished a portrait of a discontented man, of one who disturbs every happiness he possesses, from apprehension of distant evil, as any character of Congreve, or any other of our English dramatists." It has already been said that the character of Croaker was built upon a sketch by Johnson in *The Rambler*. Once when Mrs. Thrale and Miss Burney

were reading this particular paper at Streatham, Johnson
came upon them. " Ah, Madam," said he, " Goldsmith
was not scrupulous ; but he would have been a great
man, had he known the real value of his own internal
resources."

CHAPTER IX.

"THE Good Natur'd Man," we have seen, left Goldsmith the richer by £500. With this sum, it may be thought, he should have rested upon his oars, or, at all events, have raised some provisional barrier against the inroads of necessity. As it was, not being by any means an exceptional member of society, he at once invested the greater part of it in purchasing the lease of fresh chambers. His old quarters, looked at by the light of his good fortune, had grown too narrow for his importance; and he consequently moved to a second floor at No. 2, Brick Court, Middle Temple, where he had a couple of "reasonably-sized old-fashioned rooms, with a third smaller room or sleeping closet." Here he lived for the rest of his life. According to Cooke, the sum he paid for the lease was £400, and from the catalogue of the sale of his effects after his death, he must have laid out a good deal more in furnishing his new residence sumptuously. Wilton carpets, "morine festoon window-curtains compleat," Pembroke tables, "a very large dressing-glass," and his friend Sir Joshua's "Tragic Muse, in a gold frame,"—to say nothing of complete tea and card equipages—can have left but little unexpended of the balance that remained.   The step thus taken was clearly not a wise one ; and Goldsmith would have done better to respect the *Nil te quæsiveris extra* of Johnson.   For he had not only to live in his new chambers ; but he had also to live up to them ; and here began, or was further perplexed, that tangled mesh of money difficulties from which he was hardly ever afterwards to shake himself free.

In the meantime he seems to have " hung his crane " at Brick Court with all the honours.   There are traditions of suppers and dinners and card parties, at which, to use the formula of Dr. Primrose, whatever the quality of the wit, there was assuredly plenty of laughter. Blackstone, who occupied the rooms immediately below, is said to have been disturbed in the preparation of his " Commentaries " by the sounds of hilarity overhead ; and his successor, a Mr. Children, also testified to similar manifestations of the festive spirit of his neighbour above stairs.   The chief witness to these entertainments is an Irish gentleman named Seguin, who, about this date, made Goldsmith's acquaintance.   The poet was godfather to Seguin's children, and his recollections, preserved by some of these, were long afterwards communicated to Prior by a member of the family, then living in Dublin. On one especially memorable occasion the Seguins dined with Goldsmith, in company with " Mr. and Mrs. Pollard, of Castle Pollard," in order to meet Dr. Johnson.   The guests had been duly warned by their host to talk only upon such subjects as they thoroughly understood, and on no account to interrupt the great man when he had once begun to discourse.   With these precautions, added

to the favouring circumstance that "Ursa Major" chanced
to be in an unusually good temper, the evening passed
off pleasantly. Another memory represents Goldsmith
as dancing a minuet with Mrs. Seguin, a performance
which appears to have excited almost as much amusement
as the historical hornpipe of his childhood. Now and
then, it is related, he would sing Irish songs, and delight
the company with his (and Peggy Golden's) old favourite,
"The Cruelty of Barbara Allen." Here his success was
never doubtful, for, without being an accomplished vocalist,
he sang with much natural taste and feeling. At other
times, blind man's buff, forfeits, tricks with cards, and
children's games (when there were children present),
were the order of the day. "He unbent without reserve,"
says Prior, "to the level of whoever were his companions,"
and the anecdotes of this time are wholly confirmatory
of his amiability, his love of fun, and his naturally cheerful disposition. His hospitality, as may be guessed, was
in advance of his means. But it was noted that, however liberally he feasted his guests, his own habitual
evening meal was boiled milk.

In May, 1768, his elder brother ended an unobtrusive
life in his remote Irish home. Henry Goldsmith seems
to have been the only member of the family to keep up
a correspondence with his junior, whose kith and kin, by
his account, must have neglected him grievously. " I
believe I have written an hundred letters to different
friends in your country," he later tells his brother Maurice,
"and never received an answer to any of them." But for
Henry he had attempted to obtain preferment from the Earl
of Northumberland ; to Henry he had inscribed " The

Traveller " ; and to Henry he was to refer, with affectionate simplicity, in the " Dedication " of his next poem. Indeed, it is probable that the death of Henry Goldsmith, by turning his thoughts once more to the friends and home of his boyhood, stimulated the production of " The Deserted Village," in which there are undoubted traces of both. And it is admitted that at this time he began to work upon the poem. William Cooke, the young law student who wrote recollections of him in *The European Magazine*, expressly testifies to this, and gives some interesting particulars as to his methods of composition. " Goldsmith," he says, " though quick enough at prose, was rather slow in his poetry—not from the tardiness of fancy, but the time he took in pointing the sentiment and polishing the versification.[1] . . . His manner of writing poetry was this : he first sketched a part of his design in prose, in which he threw out his ideas as they occurred to him ; he then sat carefully down to versify them, and add such other ideas as he thought better fitted to the subject. He sometimes would exceed his prose design by writing several verses impromptu, but these he would take uncommon pains afterwards to revise, lest they should be found unconnected with his main design. The writer of these memoirs called upon the Doctor the second morning after he had begun ' The Deserted Village,' and to him he communicated the plan

[1] This is confirmed by others. His method, it is said, was to write his first thoughts in lines so far apart as to leave " ample room and verge enough " for copious interlineation. According to Percy, he so industriously filled these spaces with corrections that scarce a line of the original draught remained.

of his poem. . . . He then read what he had done of it that morning, beginning ' Dear lovely bowers of innocence and ease,' " and so on for ten lines. " 'Come,' says he, ' let me tell you, this is no bad morning's work ; and now, my dear boy, if you are not better engaged, I should be glad to enjoy a Shoemaker's holiday with you.' "

Assuming that Cooke is to be taken literally, the first morning's work at " The Deserted Village " must have consisted of exactly four lines, since that of the second morning begins at line five of the poem as it stands at present. But the processes of poetry are not to be so exactly meted, and it is probable that Cooke is more to be depended upon in his account of what Goldsmith calls a " shoemaker's holiday," the fashion of which was as follows : " Three or four of his [Goldsmith's] intimate friends rendezvoused at his chambers to break-fast about ten o'clock in the morning ; at eleven they proceeded by the City Road and through the fields to Highbury Barn to dinner ; about six o'clock in the evening they adjourned to White Conduit House to drink tea ; and concluded the evening by supping at the Grecian or Temple Exchange Coffee-houses, or at the Globe in Fleet Street. There was a very good ordinary of two dishes and pastry kept at Highbury Barn about this time (five and twenty years ago[1]) at 10d. per head, including a penny to the waiter, and the company generally consisted of literary characters, a few Templars, and some citizens who had left off trade. The whole expenses of this day's *fête* never exceeded a crown, and oftener from three and sixpence to four shillings, for

---

[1] Cooke wrote in 1793.

which the party obtained good air and exercise, good living, the example of simple manners, and good conversation." Prior adds a few particulars to this account, which, it may be observed, wholly neglects to include in its estimate of expenditure, the "remarkably plentiful and rather expensive breakfast," with which the proceedings began. "When finished," he says, "he [Goldsmith] had usually some poor women in attendance to whom the fragments were consigned. On one occasion, a wealthy city acquaintance, not remarkable for elegance of mind or manner, who observed this liberality, said with some degree of freedom, 'Why, Doctor, you must be a rich man; *I* cannot afford to do this.' 'It is not wealth, my dear Sir,' was the reply of the Doctor, willing to rebuke without offending his guest, 'but inclination. I have only to suppose that a few more friends than usual have been of our party, and then it amounts to the same thing.'"

Cooke, of course, frequently took part in these expeditions, and Prior enumerates some of the others who assisted. One was an original named Peter Barlow, a humble copyist in Goldsmith's employ. He always appeared in the same dress, and insisted on never paying more than fifteen pence for his dinner, the balance being made up by Goldsmith, who compensated himself with the diversion that Barlow's eccentricities afforded to the rest of the company. Another not infrequent holiday-keeper was Glover, already mentioned in connection with the "Wednesday Club." "Coley, and Williams, and Howard, and Hiff" (Hiffernan), as the line of "The Haunch of Venison" has it, were doubtless often of the

number, as well as others whose names have been forgotten
—*carent quia vate sacro.* "Our Doctor," said Glover, in
the preface to the "Poems and Plays" of 1777, "had a
constant levee of his distrest countrymen, whose wants, as
far as he was able, he always relieved ; and he has been
often known to leave himself without a guinea, in order
to supply the necessities of others." Sometimes it may
be added, he even went further than this, and borrowed
from some one else the guinea required. In Taylor's
"Records of my Life" there is a story told of Cooke to
this effect. Cooke had engaged to meet a party at
Marylebone Gardens, and applied to Goldsmith for a loan
Goldsmith had not the wherewithal ; but at once undertook to obtain it. Having waited for some time, Cooke
finally went away without the money. Returning at five
in the morning, he found it difficult to open his door ;
and, upon investigation, discovered that the obstruction
arose from a guinea wrapped in paper, which Goldsmith,
disregarding the established medium of the letter-box, had
endeavoured to thrust under it. Cooke thanked him
in the course of the day; but commented upon this unbusi-
nesslike mode of transferring funds, adding, very justly,
that any one might have found and appropriated the little
packet. "In truth, my dear fellow," replied Goldsmith,
"I did not think of that." "The fact is," adds the
charitable narrator of the anecdote, "he probably thought
of nothing but serving a friend."

From the "shoemaker's holiday" it is a natural
transition to the "Shoemaker's Paradise." This was a
summer retreat at Edgeware at the back of Canons
(Pope's "Timon's Villa"), to which Goldsmith moved

about the middle of 1768. It consisted of a tiny cottage which had been actually built for a Piccadilly shoemaker; and (by Cooke's account) was decorated in all the taste of the "Cit's Country Box" sung by Robert Lloyd, or that other and earlier civic Elysium described in No. xxxiii. of *The Connoisseur*—in other words, it included, in the "scanty plot" of half an acre, all those *jets d'eau*, flying Mercuries, gazeboes, and ditches—

> "four foot wide,
> With angles, curves, and zig-zag lines,
> From *Halfpenny's* exact designs,"

in which the common-council mind of the last century delighted when it surrendered itself to flights of fancy. Goldsmith's co-lessee of this desirable residence, was a Mr. Edmund Bott, a barrister, and author of a work on the Poor Laws, which Goldsmith is reported to have revised. Mr. Bott occupied rooms in Brick Court on the same floor as Goldsmith, and a strong friendship sprang up between them. Bott was the richer man, and Goldsmith was frequently indebted to him for loans of money; indeed, at Goldsmith's death, Bott was his chief creditor, and thus became possessor of his papers. In spite, however, of these dubious relations, they were boon companions. Edgeware, even in 1768, was not so far off as to exile them from the pleasures of the metropolis, especially in days when the orthodox dinner hour was four o'clock. Moreover, Mr. Bott kept a gig, which he drove himself—a performance not without its excitements when the charioteer was slightly in his cups. There is (or was) a letter extant in which

Goldsmith recalls how, upon one memorable occasion, his companion, having bumped a post with great dexterity, still continued to maintain doggedly that the vehicle was in the middle of the road.

It was not, however, entirely for pleasure, quickened by the " violent delight" of an occasional overturn, that Goldsmith sought the seclusion of the little cottage at the back of Lord Chandos's Edgeware mansion. During all the summer of 1768 he was, doubtless, busily employed upon the " History of Rome" he had undertaken for Davies, which was published in May of the following year. Its success was instantaneous. The charm and simplicity of the style at once caught the public, and though the writer disclaimed research, and professed only to have aimed at a school book, he obtained all the favour attaching to work that conveys instruction without making unreasonable demands on the reader's attention. Its popularity and Goldsmith's need seem speedily to have led to new enterprises of a like nature. Already, in February, 1769, he had entered into a covenant with Griffin, the publisher of the " Essays " of 1765, to write, in eight volumes, at one hundred guineas a volume, a " New Natural History of Animals," which afterwards became the well-known " Animated Nature"; and the " Roman History " was no sooner issued, than Davies made proposals for a new "English History" in four volumes *octavo*, at £500. Among Goldsmith's friends there was no doubt as to his ability to make these productions readable, even if they were not equally sure of his equipment as a naturalist or an historian. " Sir," said the ever-steadfast Johnson, "he has the art of compiling," and he predicted

that his friend would make his natural history as interesting as a Persian tale. Nowadays we may possibly
require a different standard of entertainment; but Johnson's meaning is unmistakable. Nevertheless, it is to be
regretted that necessity should have left open no other
career than "book-building" to the author of an unique
novel, an excellent comedy, and a successful didactic
poem.

Goldsmith's only contribution to the lighter muses for
the year 1769 consists of an epilogue to the comedy of
"The Sister," by Mrs. Charlotte Lennox (*née* Ramsay),
an authoress who seems to have been a considerable
favourite with the *literati* of her day. Fielding speaks of
her in his last book[1] as "the inimitable author of the
'Female Quixote,'" and Johnson was half suspected of
having revised her "Shakespeare Illustrated." It was
probably owing to this popularity that Goldsmith wrote
her the epilogue in question, as her comedy belonged to
that genteel, if not absolutely sentimental class of play,
of which he was the avowed opponent. It is a pleasant
example of his facility and good nature. The only other
incident of this year requiring record is a famous
dinner at Boswell's, which has always played an important part in all literary portraits of Goldsmith. The
impression produced by the extraordinary art of Johnson's
biographer is so vivid, that, although one feels the malice
of some of the touches, any attempt to soften them
detracts from the value of the picture. It must therefore
be given in Boswell's own words:—

---

[1] "Journal of a Voyage to Lisbon," 1755, p. 35.

" He [Johnson] honoured me with his company at dinner on the 16th October [1769], at my lodgings in Old Bond Street, with Sir Joshua Reynolds, Mr. Garrick, Dr. Goldsmith, Mr. Murphy, Mr. Bickerstaff, and Mr. Thomas Davies. Garrick played round him with a fond vivacity, taking hold of the breasts of his coat, and looking up in his face with a lively archness, complimented him on the good health which he seemed then to enjoy ; while the sage, shaking his head, beheld him with a gentle complacency. One of the company not being come at the appointed hour, I proposed, as usual upon such occasions, to order dinner to be served ; adding, ' Ought six people to be kept waiting for one ? ' ' Why, yes (answered Johnson, with a delicate humanity), if the one will suffer more by your sitting down than the six will do by waiting.' Goldsmith, to divert the tedious minutes, strutted about bragging of his dress, and I believe was seriously vain of it, for his mind was wonderfully prone to such impressions. ' Come, come, (said Garrick,) talk no more of that. You are, perhaps, the worst—eh, eh !' Goldsmith was eagerly attempting to interrupt him, when Garrick went on, laughing ironically, ' Nay, you will always *look* like a gentleman ; but I am talking of being well or *ill drest.*' ' Well, let me tell you, (said Goldsmith,) when my tailor brought home my bloom-coloured coat, he said, " Sir, I have a favour to beg of you. When anybody asks you who made your clothes, be pleased to mention John Filby, at the Harrow, in Water Lane.' *Johnson.* ' Why, sir, that was because he knew the strange colour would attract crowds to gaze at it, and thus they might hear of him, and see how well he could make a coat even of so absurd a colour.' " [1]

The conversation which followed occupies some pages of Boswell's record. But Goldsmith's part in it, or, at all events, that part which Boswell thought worthy of preservation, seems to have been confined to a curt comment on Lord Kames's "Elements of Criticism," and the not very original remark that Pope's "Atticus" showed a deep knowledge of the human heart. Johnson, on the other hand, distinguished himself more than usual, especially by his well-known and paradoxical preference of a passage in Congreve's "Mourning Bride" to anything he could recollect in Shakespeare. Not long after this memorable entertainment, simultaneous honours fell upon the two friends. *The Public Advertiser* announced that Johnson had been appointed Professor of Ancient Literature, and Goldsmith Professor of Ancient History, to the Royal Academy. This was in December; but the formal election only took place on the succeeding 9th of January. Reynolds, who had been made president some time before, was the motive power in these distinctions, which, unhappily, were purely honorary. "The King," wrote Goldsmith in January to his brother Maurice, "has lately been pleased to make me professor of Ancient History in a Royal Academy of Painting, which he has

[1] Boswell's memory errs here. The tailor's Christian name was William. Dr. Birkbeck Hill is somewhat exercised to find that Filby's accounts for this date only chronicle "bloom-coloured breeches." But Goldsmith was plainly referring to the historical suit of "Tyrian bloom, satin grain," which had been sent home just before the production of "The Good Natur'd Man."

just established, but there is no salary annexed; and I took it rather as a compliment to the institution than any benefit to myself. Honours to one in my situation are something like ruffles to one that wants a shirt." This last illustration he subsequently, after his fashion, worked into the "Haunch of Venison." In the same letter he speaks of sending to Ireland mezzotinto prints of himself, Burke, Johnson, and other of his friends. His own portrait to which he refers, was the well-known one by Reynolds, now at Knole, which was exhibited at the Royal Academy in 1770 with those of Johnson and Colman. The engraving of it by Marchi was not, however, issued until the following December, by which time Goldsmith was in possession of fresh laurels as the author of "The Deserted Village."

The poem of "The Deserted Village" had been but slowly produced. When it was at last published, on the 26th of May, 1770, nearly two years had elapsed since Cooke first found the author at work upon the opening couplets. But its reception amply atoned for any labour of the file to which it had been subjected. Before a month had passed, second, third, and fourth editions were called for, and in August came a fifth. The poem was dedicated to Reynolds, with a touching reference to Henry Goldsmith. "The only dedication I ever made was to my brother, because I loved him better than most other men. He is since dead. Permit me to inscribe this Poem to you." [1] In some passages that follow, Gold-

---

[1] Reynolds repaid this compliment in 1712, by inscribing to Goldsmith the print of " Resignation " as follows :—" This attempt

smith anticipates the objections to which he evidently felt his theory of depopulation was liable. "I sincerely believe what I have written," he said; "I have taken all possible pains, in my country excursions, for these four or five years past, to be certain of what I allege;" and "all my views and enquiries have led me to believe those miseries real, which I here attempt to display." To Cooke (unless Cooke was only paraphrasing this dedication) he spoke in similar terms. "Some of my friends," he told him, "differ with me on this plan, and think this depopulation of villages does not exist—but I am myself satisfied of the fact. I remember it in my own country, and have seen it in this." In such anxiety to show cause, there is an accent of doubt. He had, it is true, seen something of the kind in his own country, when a certain General Naper or Napier, returning enriched from Vigo, in extending his estate, displaced a number of cottiers in the neighbourhood of Lissoy. But none of his biographers have brought forward any of that evidence which he affirmed he had collected, of similar enormities in England.

There is another aspect of the poem which has proved a fertile source of speculation. What was the locality of Goldsmith's "Auburn," and how far, since other claimants may be neglected, is it to be identified with Lissoy? It has been sought to prove that Lissoy was the original Auburn, and that the likeness corresponds in the most minute particulars. This is manifestly a mistake, which

to express a character in 'The Deserted Village,' is dedicated to Doctor Goldsmith, by his sincere friend and admirer, JOSHUA REYNOLDS."

very little acquaintance with poetic methods should have sufficed to prevent. There is no evidence (although there is a vague tradition) that Goldsmith ever visited Ireland after he left it in 1752, more than fifteen years before he began to write " The Deserted Village." The poem was conceived in England; and from his desire to prove depopulation in England, was evidently intended to have its scene in England. But its leading idea was no doubt suggested by the old Napier story familiar to his boyhood, and sensibly or insensibly, for many of the accessories he drew upon his memories of his Irish home. There is no reason for supposing that, in "the decent church that topp'd the neighbouring hill," we may not recognize that of Kilkenny West as seen from Lissoy Parsonage, or that the hawthorn tree was not that imme-morial one in front of the village alehouse, which finally fell before the penknives of the curious. In the same way, the details of the alehouse itself were probably those of some kindred hostelry he had known well at Ballymahon or elsewhere. And it is certain that with the traits of the village preacher are mingled those of his father, his brother, and perhaps his Uncle Contarine, while, for the pedagogue, he obviously borrowed some of the characteristics of his old master, Thomas Byrne.

Happily, however, the popularity of "The Deserted Village" depends neither upon the fidelity of its resem-blance to a little hamlet in Westmeath, nor upon the accuracy of its theories as to luxury and depopulation. In this age, when it is not necessary, as in Goldsmith's days it was, to make declaration of some moral purpose, however doubtful, we are free to disregard its ethical and political teaching in favour of its sweet and tender cadences, and its firm hold upon the ever-fresh common-places of human nature. Johnson thought it inferior to "The Traveller," probably because it was less didactic; we, on the contrary, prefer it, because, with less obtrusion of moral, it presents in larger measure those qualities of chastened sympathy and descriptive grace which are Goldsmith at his best. It is idle to quote passages from a work so familiar. The beautiful lines, beginning, "In all my wanderings round this world of care," and the portrait of the clergyman and schoolmaster, are too well known to need recalling. But we may fitly reproduce the final farewell to Poetry, which, judging from the numerous appeals and deprecatory comments it elicited, must have excited far more apprehension among the writer's contemporaries than such valedictory addresses usually deserve. The adieus of poets, it is to be feared, are like the last appearances of actors.

> "And thou, sweet Poetry, thou loveliest maid,
> Still first to fly where sensual joys invade;
> Unfit in these degenerate times of shame,
> To catch the heart, or strike for honest fame;
> Dear charming nymph, neglected and decried,
> My shame in crowds, my solitary pride;
> Thou source of all my bliss, and all my woe,
> That found'st me poor at first, and keep'st me so;
> Thou guide by which the nobler arts excel,
> Thou nurse of every virtue, fare thee well!
> Farewell, and Oh! where'er thy voice be tried,
> On Torno's cliffs, or Pambamarca's side,
> Whether where equinoctial fervours glow,
> Or winter wraps the polar world in snow,

Still let thy voice, prevailing over time,
Redress the rigours of th' inclement clime ;
Aid slighted truth ; with thy persuasive strain
Teach erring man to spurn the rage of gain ;
Teach him, that states of native strength possess'd,
Though very poor, may still be very bless'd ;
That trade's proud empire hastes to swift decay,
As ocean sweeps the labour'd mole away ;
While self-dependent power can time defy,
As rocks resist the billows and the sky." [1]

What Goldsmith was paid for "The Deserted Village"
is uncertain. Glover says it was a hundred guineas,
and adds that Goldsmith gave the money back to his
publisher, because some one thought it was too much
Whether such a story is wholly credible, may be left to
the judicious reader to decide.

[1] The last four lines are Johnson

CHAPTER X.

AMONG the friends whom Goldsmith had made at Reynolds's house was a pleasant family from Devonshire, consisting of a mother, a son, and two daughters. The mother, Mrs. Hannah Horneck, the widow of a certain Captain Kane Horneck, of the Royal Engineers, had been known in her youth as the " Plymouth Beauty," and her daughters, Catherine and Mary, at this date girls of nineteen and seventeen respectively, inherited and even excelled her charms. Charles Horneck, the son, who had recently entered the Foot Guards, was a " pretty fellow " of sufficient eminence to be caricatured as a Macaroni ; but he was also an amiable and a genial companion. With these new acquaintances Goldsmith appears to have become very intimate, visiting them frequently at their house at Westminster, or meeting them at Sir Joshua's. There is a rhymed letter among his poems declining an invitation to join them at the house of Reynolds's physician, Dr. Baker, in which he refers to the young ladies by the pet names of " Little Comedy " and the " Jessamy Bride," while he speaks of their brother as the " Captain in Lace," titles modelled, no doubt, on the popular shop-window prints of Matthew Darly and the rest, and, whether conferred by Goldsmith or not, plainly, by their use, implying a considerable amount of familiarity.   Indeed, the personal attractions of the Miss Hornecks seem to have exercised no small fascination over the susceptible poet, a fascination to which, in the case of the younger—for Catherine was already engaged to Bunbury the caricaturist—some of his biographers have thought it justifiable to attach a gentler name.   After Catherine's marriage in August, 1771, Goldsmith was a frequent visitor at Bunbury's house at Great Barton in Suffolk, where, to this day, some relics of him, including the rhymed letter above referred to, are piously preserved.   Whether he, a mature man of forty-two, did really cherish a more than cordial friendship for the beautiful " Jessamy Bride," into whose company he was so often thrown, must be left to speculation ; but that a genuine regard existed on both sides can scarcely be contested, and many of the most interesting anecdotes of Goldsmith's latter days are derived from the recollections communicated to Prior by the lady, who, as Mrs. Gwyn, survived until 1840.

In July, 1770, shortly after the publication of a brief and not very elaborate " Life of Thomas Parnell," which he had prepared for Davies, to accompany a new edition of Parnell's works, Goldsmith set off to Paris on a holiday jaunt with Mrs. Horneck and her daughters.   "The Professor of History," writes that fair Academician, Miss Mary Moser, to Fuseli at Rome, "is comforted by the success of his ' Deserted Village,' which is a very pretty poem, and has lately put himself under the conduct of Mrs. Horneck and her fair daughters, and is gone to France ; and Dr. Johnson sips his tea, and cares not for

the vanity of the world." From Calais Goldsmith sent a
letter to Reynolds, in which he gossips brightly about
the passage, not, it appears, an entire success, owing to
the imperfect state of his "machine to prevent sea-sick-
ness." Then, after describing the extortionate civilities
of the French porters, he winds up with what is pre-
sumably a playful memory of those trivialities of travellers
which he had satirized as Lien Chi Altangi : "I cannot
help mentioning another circumstance ; I bought a new
ribbon for my wig at Canterbury, and the barber at
Calais broke it in order to gain sixpence by buying me a
new one." At Lille, where the party stopped *en route*,
occurred an incident, which, since it has been told
to Goldsmith's disadvantage, shall be given here from
the narrative of the "Jessamy Bride," as summarized
by Prior. "Having visited part of Flanders, they
were proceeding to Paris by the way of Lisle ; when in
the vicinity of the hotel at which they put up, a part of
the garrison going through some military manœuvres
drew them to the windows, when the gallantry of the offi-
cers broke forth into a variety of compliments intended
for the ears of the English ladies. Goldsmith seemed
amused ; but at length, assuming something of a severity
of countenance, which was a peculiarity of his humour
often displayed when most disposed to be jocular, turned
off, uttering something to the effect of what is commonly
stated, that elsewhere he would also have his admirers.
'This,' added my informant, 'was said in mere playful-
ness, and I was shocked many years afterwards to see it
adduced in print as a proof of his envious disposition.'"

The above disposes of the versions of Northcote and

Boswell attributing genuine jealousy to Goldsmith upon this occasion, an accusation which, as Prior says, is an absurdity, and the reference to his assumed "severity of countenance" goes far to explain some other stories of the kind. But Prior's very next sentence unconsciously confirms the charges made against him of undue pre-occupation in his own importance. "Of Paris, the same lady states, he soon became tired, the celebrity of his name and the recent success of his poem, not ensuring that attention from its literary circles which the applause received at home induced him to expect." Hence, or for some other reasons, among which may be reckoned his ill-health and pecuniary difficulties, there is little rose-colour in his next letter to Reynolds. His companions are not interested, and he himself is weary. The petty troubles of travel are harder to bear than they were when, a younger and a stronger man, he led the

> "sportive choir,
> With tuneless pipe, beside the murmuring Loire;"

the diet disagrees with his dyspepsia, and he is hungering for tidings of Johnson, and Burke, and Colman, and the rest of the Gerrard Street company. He has besides, he says, "so outrun the constable that he must mortify a little to bring it up again;" and he has bought a silk coat which makes him look like a fool. So the letter ambles on to the close. He cannot say more because he intends showing it to the ladies, and he concludes with a phrase beginning with a pair of words almost as common on his lips as his favourite "In truth"—"What signifies teasing you longer with moral observations when the business of my writing is over?" He has only one thing more to say, and of that he thinks every hour, that he is his correspondent's most sincere and most affectionate friend." It has been hinted that to his other continental discomforts was added an uncongenial companion, Mr. Hickey of "Retaliation," who joined the party, and being familiar with Paris, absorbed too much attention. Hickey was, as Goldsmith called him afterwards, "a most blunt, pleasant creature," but at this time the former qualification seems to have been in the ascendant. The two men, in short, did not agree, and to this circumstance, perhaps, are to be traced one or two of the less creditable anecdotes of the poet dating from this time. While at Versailles, it is said, Goldsmith, remembering his old prowess as a boy, attempted to leap from the bank on to one of the little islets, and fell lamentably short. Doubtless this (as Prior says), "was to the great amusement of the company" (and probably to the detriment of the silk coat); but it is manifestly an episode that may be told in many ways, according to the taste and fancy of the teller. In Mr. Hickey's unsympathetic narrative, for instance, it would probably acquire all the advantages of picturesque treatment.

In his letter to Reynolds, touching that little sentence about "outrunning the constable," Goldsmith had spoken of laying by at Dover, or rather of taking a country lodging in the vicinity, "in order to do some business." When his six weeks' excursion was over, however, he does not appear to have acted upon his intention, perhaps because of the death of his mother, of which he had received intelligence while abroad. There is a silly story, repeated by Northcote, that he only put on half-mourning for this bereavement. But it has been refuted by both Prior and Forster, with the aid of Mr. Filby's bills, which duly record the purchase of a suit of mourning sent home on the 8th of September, and the terms are identical with those which chronicle similar purchases made upon the deaths of his brother Henry and the Princess Dowager of Wales. Probably the expense thus incurred served to increase the activity with which he returned to the old task work. Only a few days after Mr. Filby sent home the new clothes, Goldsmith had agreed with Davies to abridge the " Roman History " of the previous year for fifty guineas, and, even before entering upon this labour, he was engaged upon another task for the same bookseller, a life of Bolingbroke, intended to introduce a reprint of that writer's " Dissertation upon Parties." The book must have been hastily prepared, for it was published in December, without any author's name ; and, from one of Davies' letters to Granger of the " Biographical History," apparently took as much time to print as to write. " Doctor Goldsmith," he complains, "is gone with Lord Clare into the country, and I am plagued to get the proofs from him of his ' Life of Lord Bolingbroke.' " The evidences of hurry were more manifest in this work than usual, and his old enemies of *The Monthly Review* did not fail to make merry over its errors of the pen, and its sporadic Johnsonese. But his facts are said to have been fully abreast of contemporary knowledge ; and he had, at least, one quality of success—that of genuine admiration for the parts and politics of the brilliant genius who formed his subject.

As already stated, the book was issued in December, and from Davies' words it is clear that Goldsmith had already gone to visit Lord Clare before this date. He stayed with him some time, and during the opening months of 1771 was still in his company. "Goldsmith is at Bath, with Lord Clare," writes Johnson to Langton, in March. At Bath occurred that characteristic second visit to the Duke of Northumberland,[1] which, since it is related by Percy on the authority of the Duchess herself, can scarcely be rejected by the courteous biographer, even if it were not, as it is, an incident thoroughly in keeping with what we know of Goldsmith from other sources. "On one of the parades at Bath," says Percy, " the Duke and Lord Nugent had hired two adjacent houses. Dr. Goldsmith, who was then resident on a visit to the latter, one morning walked up into the Duke's dining-room, as he and the Duchess were preparing to sit down to breakfast. In a manner the most free and easy he threw himself on a sofa; and as he was then perfectly known to them both, they inquired of him the Bath news of the day ; and, imagining there was some mistake, endeavoured by easy and cheerful conversation to prevent his being too much embarrassed, till breakfast being served up, they invited him to stay and partake of it. Then he awoke from his reverie, declared he thought he had been in the house of his friend Lord Nugent, and with a confusion which may be imagined, hastily withdrew ; but not till they had kindly made him promise to dine with them."

That Goldsmith referred to his friend as Lord Nugent

[1] See Chapter VII. The Earl of Northumberland had been created a Duke in 1766.

is scarcely possible, for Lord Clare did not obtain this
title until after Goldsmith had been dead two years.
This, however, is a trifle which detracts little from the
veracity of the story.   How much longer he continued to
be Lord Clare's guest is unrecorded; but shortly after his
return to London he is supposed to have addressed to
him, in return for a present of venison, the delightful
"poetical epistle" which is to be found in his works.
That it was written subsequent to the middle of 1770
may be inferred from its quotation of a famous lapse [1] in
one of the love-letters of his illiterate Royal Highness,
Henry Frederick, Duke of Cumberland, to the Countess
Grosvenor—a correspondence which, in the summer of
the above year, afforded huge delight to the scandal-
mongers—and it is most probable that the poem was
written in the spring of 1771.   But whatever its exact
date, Mr. Forster is right (notwithstanding a slight ob
scurity in the closing lines) in claiming the highest praise
for this piece of " private pleasantry."   So happy is it, that,
were it not for its obvious recollections of Boileau's third
satire, one might be disposed to regard it as autobiogra-
phical.   To select a passage from a piece so uniformly
wrought is difficult, but the excellence of the description
of the dinner, as a sample of what his most superfine
contemporaries called the poet's " low " humour, must
serve as an excuse for quoting it at length.   The reader
will only need to remember that while Goldsmith, having

---

[1] " Left alone to reflect, having emptied my shelf,
' And nobody with me at sea but myself.' "
The second line is almost a textual reproduction of a phrase in one
of the Duke's letters.

distributed part of his just-received present, is debating
what to do with the rest, it is unblushingly carried off by
a chance visitor, who invites its owner to join in eating
it in the form of a pasty :—

> "When come to the place where we all were to dine,
> (A chair-lumber'd closet just twelve feet by nine :)
> My friend bade me welcome, but struck me quite dumb,
> With tidings that Johnson and Burke would not come ;
> 'For I knew it,' he cried, 'both eternally fail,
> The one with his speeches, and t'other with Thrale ;
> But no matter, I'll warrant we'll make up the party
> With two full as clever, and ten times as hearty.
> The one is a Scotchman, the other a Jew,
> They['re] both of them merry and authors like you ;
> The one writes the *Snarler*, the other the *Scourge ;*
> Some think he writes *Cinna*—he owns to *Panurge.*'
> While thus he describ'd them by trade and by name,
> They enter'd, and dinner was serv'd as they came.
>
> At the top a fried liver and bacon were seen,
> At the bottom was tripe in a swinging tureen ;
> At the sides there was spinage and pudding made hot ;
> In the middle a place where the pasty—was not.
> Now, my Lord, as for tripe, it's my utter aversion,
> And your bacon I hate like a Turk or a Persian ;
> So there I sat stuck, like a horse in a pound,
> While the bacon and liver went merrily round.
> But what vex'd me most was that d——'d Scottish rogue,
> With his long-winded speeches, his smiles, and his brogue ;
> And, 'Madam,' quoth he, 'may this bit be my poison,
> A prettier dinner I never set eyes on ;
> Pray a slice of your liver, though may I be curs'd,
> But I've eat of your tripe till I'm ready to burst.'
> 'The tripe,' quoth the Jew, with his chocolate cheek,
> 'I could dine on this tripe seven days in the week :
> I like these here dinners so pretty and small ;
> But your friend there, the Doctor, eats nothing at all.'

' O—Oh !' quoth my friend, ' he'll come on in a trice,
He's keeping a corner for something that's nice :
There's a pasty '—' A pasty !' repeated the Jew,
' I don't care if I keep a corner for't too.'
' What the de'il, mon, a pasty !' re-echoed the Scot,
' Though splitting, I'll still keep a corner for thot.'
' We'll all keep a corner,' the lady cried out ;
' We'll all keep a corner,' was echoed about.
While thus we resolv'd, and the pasty delay'd,
With looks that quite petrified, entered the maid ;
A visage so sad, and so pale with affright,
Wak'd Priam in drawing his curtains by night.
But we quickly found out, for who could mistake her?
That she came with some terrible news from the baker :
And so it fell out, for that negligent sloven
Had shut out the pasty on shutting his oven."

As a piece of graphic, easy humour Goldsmith has not
often bettered this. The references to Johnson and
Burke, the side-strokes (perfectly perceptible to Lord
Clare) at Parson Scott in " Cinna " and " Panurge," the
vulgar effusiveness of the hungry North Briton, and
the neat fidelity of the Jew's " I like these here
dinners so pretty and small "—are all perfect in their
way. Nor should the skill with which Goldsmith
manages to suggest that he is " among " but not " of "
the company, be overlooked. Indeed, it would, in some
respects, be more difficult to match a passage of this
kind than anything in "The Traveller" or " The Deserted
Village."[1]

[1] At this point Mr. Forster interposes an account of an undated
translation by Goldsmith of Marco Vida's " Game of Chess," first
published by Cunningham in 1854 from the original MS. in the
possession of Mr. Bolton Corney. It is written in heroic measure ;
but makes no particular addition to Goldsmith's poetical reputation.

On the 24th of August, 1770 (when Goldsmith was at
Paris with the Hornecks), Thomas Chatterton had committed suicide in his Holborn garret, and one of the topics
of conversation at the first dinner of the Royal Academy
on the 23rd of April, 1771 (St. George's Day), was his
genius and his untimely fate. From a memorandum
afterwards drawn up by Horace Walpole, it seems that
Goldsmith was one of the believers in the Rowley poems.
" I thought no more," says Walpole, referring to his
intercourse with the Bristol genius, " of him or them
[his poems] till about a year and a half after, when,
dining at the Royal Academy, Dr. Goldsmith drew
the attention of the company with the account of a
marvellous treasure of ancient poems lately discovered
at Bristol, and expressed enthusiastic belief in them,
for which he was laughed at by Dr. Johnson, who
was present. I soon found this to be the *trouvaille*
of my friend Chatterton, and I told Dr. Goldsmith that
this novelty was known to me, who might, if I had
pleased, have had the honour of ushering the great discovery to the learned world. You may imagine, sir, we
did not at all agree in the measure of our faith; but
though his credulity diverted me, my mirth was soon
dashed ; for on asking about Chatterton, he told me he
had been to London, and had destroyed himself. The
persons of honour and veracity who were present will
attest with what surprise and concern I thus first heard
of his death." Goldsmith, upon another occasion, took
up the cudgels for the poems against Percy so hotly, that
Percy, who had much of the Northumberland temper,
retorted with equal warmth, and a breach ensued, which

was not at once repaired. The only other anecdote with respect to this matter relates that Goldsmith was at one time anxious to become the purchaser of the Rowley MSS. But as the only consideration proposed was a promissory note, Mr. George Catcott, their possessor, replied drily that a poet's note of hand would scarcely pass current on the Bristol Exchange.

Shortly after his return from Lord Clare's, Goldsmith, under pressure of literary labour, again resorted to the solitude of the country. He took a room in a farmhouse near the six-mile stone on the Edgeware Road, carrying down his books in two returned post-chaises. This room, says Prior, he continued to use as a summer residence until his death, and here great part of his " Animated Nature," his " History of Greece " and other later compilations was written. It was an airy chamber up one pair of stairs, looking cheerfully over a wooded landscape towards Hendon, and when visited by Boswell and Mickle of the " Lusiads " in the following year, was found to be scrawled all over with " curious scraps of descriptions of animals." Such memories of Goldsmith at this date as survive, represent him wandering in the fields, or musing under hedges, or now and then taking his station abstractedly in front of Farmer Selby's kitchen fire. Often he would depart suddenly for Brick Court, where he would remain for a week or more. On other occasions a dance would be improvised, or he would treat the younger members of the family to the diversion of the strolling players. At intervals he was visited by some of his London friends. Reynolds, Chambers, and even Johnson are believed to have been thus entertained, upon which occasions of

state he migrated to his landlord's parlour. By the
farmer's family he was known as "The Gentleman," and
was regarded as slightly eccentric. But here, as every-
where, the recollection of his kindliness and generosity
lingered in men's minds. No tramp or beggar ever
applied to him in vain.

In August, 1771, the "History of England" was published, and to this and another work upon which he had
been engaged he refers in a letter addressed from the
Temple to Bennet Langton, "at Langton, near Spilsby, in
Lincolnshire," and dated the 17th of the following September. "I have published, or Davies has published
for me," he says, "an Abridgment of the History of
England, for which I have been a good deal abused in
the newspapers, for betraying the liberties of the people.
God knows I had no thought for or against liberty in my
head; my whole aim being to make up a book of a
decent size, that, as 'Squire Richard says, would do no
harm to nobody. However, they set me down as an
arrant Tory, and consequently an honest man. When
you come to look at any part of it, you'll say that I am a
sour Whig." On other of his occupations also the letter
throws light. The "Natural History," he says, is about
half-finished; and he will shortly finish the rest, he adds,
with a sigh over "this kind of finishing," and his "scurvy
circumstances." But he has been doing something—he
has for the last three months been trying "to make
people laugh." He has been strolling about the hedges,
"studying jests with the most tragical countenance."
This, with another passage at the beginning of the letter,
in which he says he has "been almost wholly in the

country at a farmer's house, quite alone, trying to write a comedy," is the first indication of his having again turned his attention to the stage. The new play was now finished, but when or how it would be acted, or whether it would be acted at all, were questions he could not resolve.

The occurrences which intervened between its completion and production may be rapidly abridged. One of the occasional pieces of this date was a prologue to "Zobeide," a translation or adaptation of an unfinished tragedy by Voltaire called "Les Scythes." Its author was a gentleman of Leicestershire named Joseph Cradock, who, about this time, had been introduced to Goldsmith by Yates, the actor, and maintained a fast friendship for him during the remainder of his life—a friendship concerning which Cradock, in his old age, published some rather mythical recollections. In February, 1772, the death of the Princess Dowager of Wales prompted Goldsmith, for some unexplained reason, to prepare a lament-to-order, which he entitled "Threnodia Augustalis." It was sung and recited at the famous Mrs. Cornelys' in Soho Square, but has little more than the merit of opportunism, and was very hastily composed. Between these two comes, in all probability, the lively letter in prose and verse to Catherine Horneck, now Mrs. Bunbury of Barton, first published by Prior in 1837, from the Bunbury papers. Under cover of a reply to an invitation to spend Christmas in the country, the letter goes off into a charming piece of rhyming banter, in which Mrs. Bunbury and her sister are arraigned at the Old Bailey for giving disingenuous counsel to the poet at Loo :—

" Both are placed at the bar, with all proper decorum,
    With bunches of fennel and nosegays before 'em ; [1]
    Both cover their faces with mobs and all that,
    But the judge bids them, angrily, take off their hat.
    When uncover'd, a buzz of inquiry runs round—
    ' Pray what are their crimes ? '—' They've been pilfering found.'
    ' But, pray, who[m] have they pilfer'd ? '—' A doctor, I hear.'
    ' What, yon solemn-faced, odd-looking man that stands near ! '
    ' The same.'—' What a pity ! how does it surprise one,
    Two handsomer culprits I never set eyes on ! '
    Then their friends all come round me with cringing and leering,
    To melt me to pity, and soften my swearing.
    First Sir Charlés'advances with phrases well strung,
    ' Consider, dear Doctor, the girls are but young ; '
    ' The younger the worse,' I return him again,
    ' It shows that their habits are all dyed in grain.'
    ' But then they're so handsome, one's bosom it grieves.'
    ' What signifies *handsome*, when people are thieves ? '
    ' But where is your justice ? their cases are hard.'
    ' What signifies *justice ?*   I want the reward.' "

And then the letter, with its ingenuity of compliment,
heightened by the touch as to that "solemn-faced, odd-
looking man," the writer, drops into parish-beadle recitative
and ends :—

" ' But consider their case,—it may yet be your own !
    And see how they kneel ! Is your heart made of stone ? '
    This moves :—so at last I agree to relent,
    For ten pounds in hand, and ten pounds to be spent."

I challenge you all to answer this : I tell you, you cannot. It cuts
deep ;—but now for the rest of the letter : and next—but I want
room—so I believe I shall battle the rest out at Barton some day
next week.   " I don't value you all !
                                               "O. G."

----

[1] A practice dating from the gaol-fever of 1750. Compare the
Old Bailey scene in Cruikshank's "Drunkard's Children," 1848,
plate v.

By this time, retouched and revised, the comedy of which Goldsmith had written to Langton, was in Colman's hands. Unhappily, in Colman's hands it remained. At the end of 1772 he had not made up his mind whether he would say " yes " or " no " to Goldsmith's repeated applications for his decision—applications which the poet's necessities made upon each occasion more importunate. In January, 1773, referring to these, he pressed urgently for a final reply. He petitioned for at least the same measure which had been given to " as bad plays as his," and he even humbled himself so far as to offer to make alterations. Thereupon Colman took him at his word, and suggested numerous frivolous amendments, under the momentary irritation of which the smarting poet offered the manuscript to Garrick, withdrawing it again as speedily. Then stout old Johnson took the matter up, using the strongest persuasions (even " a kind of force ") to Colman, the result being that a definite promise to produce the play was at length wrung from that potentate, although against his judgment. " Dr. Goldsmith," wrote Johnson shortly afterwards, " has a new comedy in rehearsal at Covent Garden, to which the manager predicts ill-success. I hope he will be mistaken. I think it deserves a very kind reception."

The production at the Haymarket in February of Foote's famous Primitive Puppet Show of the "Handsome Housemaid ; or, Piety in Pattens," which certainly counts as an important factor in the story of the crusade against sentimental comedy, opportunely aided in preparing the popular taste. But the fates were, even now, too much against Goldsmith to make his success an easy one. The prejudice of Colman communicated itself to the company, and one after another of the leadin· actors threw up their parts. That of the first gentleman fell to Lee Lewes, the theatrical harlequin, while the best character in the piece was assigned to Quick, who, in "The Good Natur'd Man," had filled no more important office than that of a post-boy. Fresh troubles arose respecting the epilogue, of which no less than four different versions were written, in consequence of objections raised by the manager and the actresses. Finally, until a few days before the play appeared, it was still without a name. Reynolds advocated "The Belle's Stratagem," a title afterwards used by Mrs. Cowley; some one else "The Old House a New Inn," which certainly summarized the main idea, borrowed from Goldsmith's Ardagh experiences as narrated in chapter i.; while for some time "The Mistakes of a Night" found a measure of favour. Then Goldsmith, perhaps remembering, as Mr. Forster suggests, a line from Dryden, fixed upon "She Stoops to Conquer," to which "The Mistakes of a Night" was added as a sub-title. On the 15th of March, 1773, the play was acted at Covent Garden, and a few days afterwards published in book form, with a dedication to its firm friend, Johnson. "I do not mean," wrote the grateful author, "so much to compliment you as myself. It may do me some honour to inform the public, that I have lived many years in intimacy with you. It may serve the interests of mankind also to inform them, that the greatest wit may be found in a character, without impairing the most unaffected piety."

To the very last Colman maintained his unhopeful attitude, in spite of the steady enthusiasm of the author's friends, who, after dining together at a tavern, had, under Johnson's generalship, proceeded in a body to the theatre, determined to make a stubborn fight for the piece. But, according to the best accounts, there was no necessity for any advocacy, hostile or otherwise, for, "quite the reverse to everybody's expectation," the play was received "with the utmost applause." Even Horace Walpole, who sneered aristocratically at its "lowness," and wrote flippantly about the author's draggled Muse, could not deny that it "succeeded prodigiously." "All eyes," he told Lady Ossory, "were upon Johnson, who sat in a front row in a side box; and when he laughed, everybody thought himself warranted to roar." In the mean time, the poor author, who had not dared to accompany his party to Covent Garden, was wandering disconsolately in the Mall. Here he was discovered by a friend, who pointed out to him that, in the event of any sudden alterations being required, his absence from the theatre might have serious results, and prevailed upon him to go there. "He entered the stage door," Cooke tells us, "just in the middle of the fifth Act, when there was a hiss at the improbability of Mrs. Hardcastle supposing herself forty miles off, though on her own grounds, and near the house. 'What's that?' says the Doctor, terrified at the sound. 'Psha! Doctor,' says Colman, who was standing by the side of the scene, 'don't be fearful of *squibs*, when we have been sitting almost these two hours upon a barrel of gunpowder." Goldsmith, adds Cooke, never forgave Colman this gratuitous piece of malice.

The success of "She Stoops to Conquer" was thoroughly deserved. It was an immense improvement upon its predecessor. Compared with Croaker and Lofty, Tony Lumpkin and Mr. Hardcastle are as characters to characteristics, while Mrs. Hardcastle, Hastings, Young Marlowe, Miss Hardcastle, and Miss Neville, are far beyond the Honeywoods and Richlands of "The Good Natur'd Man." Whatever there may be of farcical in the plot, vanished before the hearty laughter that the piece raised on its first appearance, and has raised ever since. " I know of no comedy for many years (said Johnson) that has answered so much the great end of comedy—making an audience merry." That such an inexhaustible bequest of mirth should have come to us from a man tortured with nervous apprehensions, and struggling with money difficulties, is a triumphant testimony to the superiority of genius over circumstance. It is consolatory to think that, in spite of every obstacle, "She Stoops to Conquer" was acted for many nights, and, besides being twice commanded by royalty itself brought its author, at his benefits, the more substantial gratification of some four or five hundred pounds, to which must be added a further amount from the publication of the play in book form.

CHAPTER XI.

WHILE the "newspaper witlings and pert scribbling folks" vied with each other in exulting over the glorious defeat, by " She Stoops to Conquer," of the allied forces of sentimental comedy, and amused themselves by planting arrowy little epigrams in the sides of Mr. Manager Colman and Mr. Staymaker Kelly, insomuch that the former implored the author "to take him off the rack of the newspapers," there were not wanting those who, on the other hand, essayed to disparage Goldsmith himself. In *The London Packet* of the 24th of March appeared a letter signed "Tom Tickle," headed by the motto " *Vous vous noyez par vanité*," and attacking him venomously at all points. He was charged with puffing his own productions : his " Traveller " was said to be "a flimsy poem, built upon false principles ;" his "Good Natur'd Man," a " poor, water-gruel, dramatic dose ;" his " Deserted Village," " easy numbers, without fancy, dignity, genius, or fire ; " and " She Stoops to Conquer," a " speaking pantomime " and " an incoherent piece of stuff." Lastly, he was enjoined to " reduce his vanity," and to endeavour to believe that, as a man, he " was of the plainest sort ; and as an author, but a mortal piece of mediocrity."

There is little doubt that the dealer of this stab in the dark was Goldsmith's old enemy, Kenrick, and the mere abuse which it contained was of little moment. But towards the beginning of the letter, where Goldsmith is accused of being a very Narcissus for pleased contemplation of his personal advantages, it goes on : " Was but the lovely H——k as much enamoured, you would not sigh, my gentle swain, in vain." This, it must be admitted, was unpardonable, and Goldsmith was justly indignant. According to Cradock, to make matters worse, he dined with the Hornecks in Westminster almost immediately after they had read the article, and found them all greatly disturbed. Dinner being over, he went straight to the shop of the publisher, a Welshman named Evans, in Paternoster Row, accompanied, says one account, by the lady's brother, Captain Horneck, or, says another, by that Captain Higgins who, in the " Haunch of Venison," is celebrated "for making a blunder, or picking a bone." Mr. Forster thinks that Higgins is most likely to have been the poet's companion ; but if Cradock's statement as to his dining with the family is true, it is surely not improbable that he should have gone with Captain Horneck. However, what happened at the shop was communicated to Prior by an eye-witness, Evans's assistant, Mr. Harris. Being asked by the two gentlemen whether Evans was at home, he says : " I called the latter from an adjoining room, and heard Goldsmith say to him—'I have called in consequence of a scurrilous attack in your paper upon me (my name is Goldsmith), and an unwarrantable liberty taken with the name of a young lady. As for myself, I care little, but

her name must not be sported with.' Evans, declaring
his ignorance of the matter, said he would speak to the
editor, and stooping down for the file of the paper to
look for the offensive article, the poet struck him smartly
with his cane across the back. Evans, who was sturdy,
returned the blow with interest, when, in the scuffle, a
lamp suspended overhead was broken, and the oil fell
upon the combatants; one of the shopmen was sent for
a constable, but in the meantime Dr. Kenrick, who had
been all the time in the adjoining room, and who, it was
pretty certain, was really author of the newspaper article,
came forward, separated the parties, and sent Goldsmith
home in a coach. Captain Horneck expressed his surprise at the assault, declaring he had no previous intima-
tion of such a design on the part of the poet, who had
merely requested that he should accompany him to
Paternoster Row. Evans took steps to indict him for
an assault; but subsequently a compromise took place
by his assailant agreeing to pay fifty pounds to a Welsh
charity." This, however, was not effected until after
Goldsmith had written a dignified letter to *The Daily
Advertiser* on the "licentiousness" of the press, which,
as may be supposed, made itself very merry over his
misadventure. Silence would, no doubt, have been
wiser; but even Johnson was obliged to admit that
the letter was "a foolish thing well done."

But from Goldsmith scuffling with a bookseller under
a cataract of lamp-oil — certainly a most ill-advised
mode of "stooping to conquer," as the wits did not
fail to remind him—it is pleasant to turn to Goldsmith
chatting and chirrupping in the company of his friends.

A week or two later Boswell gives an account of a dinner at General Oglethorpe's with " Dr. *Major*" and " Dr. *Minor*," when Goldsmith held forth on his favourite theme of luxury and the consequent degeneration of the race—a position which Johnson contested. After dinner they drank tea with the ladies, to whom Goldsmith sang Tony Lumpkin's capital song of the "Three Jolly Pigeons," and the pretty quatrains ("Ah me, when shall I marry me?") to the tune of the "Humours of Balama- gairy," which Boswell published some years later in *The London Magazine.* Moore also used the air in the "Irish Melodies;" but scarcely as happily as Goldsmith, and it is to be regretted that the song had to be omitted from "She Stoops to Conquer" because Mrs. Bulkley (who played Miss Hardcastle) could not sing. Goldsmith himself, says Boswell, sang it very agreeably. Two days later the trio met again at General Paoli's. Boswell chronicles a long conversation, the only portion of which can have a place here is a compliment by the General to Goldsmith. Paoli referred to a passage in "She Stoops to Conquer" which was supposed, rightly or wrongly, to make oblique allusion to the recent marriage of the Duke of Gloucester and Lady Waldegrave.[1] That "literary leech," Boswell, ever on the watch for *ana*, forthwith attempted to entice Goldsmith into an admission of this intention. He smiled and hesitated in his usual way; and the General came to his aid. " *Monsieur Goldsmith est comme la mer, qui jette des perles et beaucoup d'autres*

---

[1] See Act ii., where Hastings says : "If my dearest girl will trust in her faithful Hastings, we shall soon be landed in France, where even among slaves the laws of marriage are respected."

belles choses, sans s'en apercevoir." Goldsmith was highly delighted. " *Très bien dit et très élégamment,*" was his flattered comment. There was another dinner at Thrale's still later ; but it can have no record in these pages.

In August his gratitude to Shuter for his presentment of Tony Lumpkin prompted him to adapt for that actor's benefit a dull play by Brueys and Palaprat, "Le Grondeur," which he shortened into a farce under the title of " The Grumbler." It was produced at Covent Garden on the 8th of May ; but never received the honours of repetition. Prior included a scene from it in the "Miscellaneous Works" of 1837, and it is generally reprinted with the author's other plays. But, although from a note written in this year to Garrick, he appears to have been still dreaming of a future comedy, " in a season or two at furthest," which he fancied he should make a fine thing, he was hopelessly in bondage to the hack work by which he lived. In the intervals of the " Animated Nature" he had been engaged with a " Grecian History," for which, in June, 1773, upon the completion of the first volume, he received £250 from Griffin, probably a nominal payment only, as he was in debt to the publisher for arrears already due. He also meditated a popular " Dictionary of Arts and Sciences," of which he was to be editor, with Johnson, Reynolds, Burke, Burney, Garrick, and all his friends as contributors. For this he drew up an elaborate prospectus, said by Cradock and others to be excellently conceived, but no longer known to exist. The booksellers, however, shrank from so large an enterprise, and the matter made no progress. Perhaps, too, as Davies and others suggest, they distrusted the organizing capacity of a worker so needy, so overburdened, and so irregular in his habits. Queer errors sometimes made their appearance in his rapidly written books. There had been such in his histories, and an anecdote is told by Dawson Turner which shows that he must often have been hasty as to his authorities. Once, when engaged on the " History of Greece," he asked Gibbon the name of the Indian king who gave Alexander so much trouble, and when Gibbon jestingly answered, " Montezuma," he had to correct himself immediately lest Goldsmith should commit the statement to type.

In the collapse of the Dictionary scheme his thoughts reverted to " The Good Natur'd Man," and he wrote to Garrick offering to recast that comedy, at the same time asking for a loan. Garrick lent the money ; but did not accept the proposal, which he labelled " Goldsmith's parlaver " and put away. After this there is not much to relate in Goldsmith's life, which, notwithstanding the growing burden of breaking health and increased embarrassment, seems still to have had its delights. There are glimpses of him at Drury Lane on the first night of Kelly's comedy of the " School for Wives ;" at Beauclerk's with Garrick, making an entire company shriek with laughter over some pantomimic buffoonery ; at Vauxhall with Sir Joshua. " Sir Joshua and Goldsmith," writes Beauclerk, as late as February, 1774, " have got into such a round of pleasures that they have no time." And in these last days an accident brought about the composition of one of his cleverest pieces, which, although never completed, will probably be remembered as long as " The Deserted Village." According to the now accepted story, a party at the St. James's Coffee-house, prompted thereto by some gasconade of Goldsmith, fell into the whim of writing competitive epitaphs upon him. Garrick led off with the well-known impromptu :

> " Here lies Nolly Goldsmith, for shortness called Noll,
> Who wrote like an angel, but talked like poor Poll ; "

and others followed. Goldsmith, rather disconcerted by the ready applause which followed Garrick's neat anti-thesis, deferred the revenge which he was invited to take, and continued to work desultorily at his reply until a few days before his death, shortly after which it was published by Kearsly under the name of " Retaliation : Including Epitaphs on the Most Distinguished Wits of the Metropolis." By a recollection of the famous picnic dinners of Scarron (whose " Roman Comique," among other hack-work, he had just been translating), he began with likening his friends to dishes, but speedily wound into that incomparable series of epigrammatic portraits which is to-day one of the most graphic picture-galleries of his immediate contemporaries. Johnson is con-spicuously absent, perhaps because, though one of the company, he had not joined in the initial attack,—perhaps, also, because the poem is unfinished ; but Burke, Rey-nolds, Cumberland, and Garrick are admirably portrayed. Between these, in point of literary art, there is little to choose, unless the mingling of satire, compliment, and faithful characterization is held to reach its acme in the admirable lines on Garrick :—

" Here lies David Garrick, describe me, who can,
An abridgment of all that was pleasant in man ;
As an actor, confess'd without rival to shine :
As a wit, if not first, in the very first line :
Yet, with talents like these, and an excellent heart,
The man had his failings, a dupe to his art.
Like an ill-judging beauty, his colours he spread,
And beplaster'd with rouge his own natural red.
On the stage he was natural, simple, affecting ;
'Twas only that when he was off he was acting.
With no reason on earth to go out of his way,
He turn'd and he varied full ten times a day.
Though secure of our hearts, yet confoundedly sick
If they were not his own by finessing and trick :
He cast off his friends, as a huntsman his pack,
For he knew when he pleas'd he could whistle them back.
Of praise a mere glutton, he swallow'd what came,
And the puff of a dunce he mistook it for fame ;
Till his relish grown callous, almost to disease,
Who pepper'd the highest was surest to please.
But let us be candid, and speak out our mind,
If dunces applauded, he paid them in kind.
Ye Kenricks, ye Kellys, and Woodfalls so grave,
What a commerce was yours, while you got and you gave !
How did Grub Street re-echo the shouts that you rais'd,
While he was be-Roscius'd, and you were be-prais'd !
But peace to his spirit, wherever it flies,
To act as an angel, and mix with the skies :
Those poets, who owe their best fame to his skill,
Shall still be his flatterers, go where he will.
Old Shakespeare, receive him, with praise and with love,
And Beaumonts and Bens be his Kellys above ! "

"The sum of all that can be said for and against Mr
Garrick, some people think, may be found in these lines
of Goldsmith," wrote Thomas Davies. When Garrick's
own biographer is obliged to admit so much, there can

be little doubt of the accuracy of the portrait. Next in importance to this, composed in an inimitable spirit of irony, comes the sketch of Cumberland, which, in his old age, that writer seems to have grown to regard as entirely complimentary. Burke's character, too, contains some famous couplets, seldom forgotten when his name is recalled. But the most delightful, because the most wholly genial and kindly, of the epitaphs, is that upon Reynolds :—

> " Here Reynolds is laid, and, to tell you my mind,
>   He has not left a better or wiser behind :
>   His pencil was striking, resistless, and grand ;
>   His manners were gentle, complying, and bland ;
>   Still born to improve us in every part,
>   His pencil our faces, his manners our heart :
>   To coxcombs averse, yet most civilly steering,
>   When they judg'd without skill he was still hard of hearing :
>   When they talked of their Raphaels, Correggios, and stuff,
>   He shifted his trumpet, and only took snuff."

Malone says that half a line more had been written when Goldsmith dropped the pen ; and Prior, who gives the words as " By flattery unspoiled," affirms that, among several erasures in the manuscript, they " remained unaltered." To the fifth edition was appended a " Postscript," containing a supplementary epitaph on Caleb Whitefoord, who had also been one of the party at the St. James's Coffee-house, and was the inventor of the famous " Cross-Readings," which proved so popular *circa* 1766–70. It presents some of Goldsmith's peculiarities and negligences ; but is not entirely free from the suspicion that Whitefoord wrote it himself.

The appearance of " Retaliation " brought about a number of *ex post facto* epitaphs, most of which, in all probability, their writers would have been pleased to pass off as the original productions to which Goldsmith had been invited to reply. Garrick, who wrote the best of these (" Here, Hermes ! says Jove, who with nectar was mellow "), at one time meditated their publication ; but his intention was never carried out, and, as already stated, Goldsmith's death took place before " Retaliation " was given to the world. Still working at that poem, and still planning fresh compilations which were to enable him to cope with his difficulties, he had gone again to his Edgeware home, when a sharp attack of a local disorder, induced by his sedentary habits, obliged him to seek medical advice in town. To London he accordingly returned in the middle of March. He saw a doctor, and obtained relief. But low fever supervened, and on the 25th (one of the club Fridays) he took to his bed. At eleven at night he sent for a surgeon-apothecary in the Strand named Hawes,[1] who found him extremely ill, but bent upon curing himself by Dr. James's Fever Powders, a patent medicine upon which he had been accustomed to rely. Hawes did not think it suited to his condition, which was more nervous than febrile, and

---

[1] William Hawes, who afterwards wrote " An Account of the late Dr. Goldsmith's Illness, etc.," was the grandfather of Sir Benjamin Hawes, once Under-Secretary at War. He undertook the active management of Goldsmith's affairs pending the arrival of his relatives from Ireland, and arranged the sale of the books, &c. Goldsmith's writing-desk, which belonged to Hawes, is now in the South Kensington Museum.

endeavoured to induce him to try other remedies.
Failing in this, he persuaded him to send for a physician, Dr. Fordyce, who confirmed his view of the case.
Goldsmith, however, still clung obstinately to James's
nostrum, and rejected the medicine prescribed by Dr
Fordyce. After taking the powder he became worse,
and was obliged to resign himself to the advice of those
about him. Becoming exceedingly weak and sleepless,
he lingered for a week longer in a state that caused the
gravest anticipations, although he was conscious, and
sometimes (it is said) even cheerful. Dr. Turton, a
second physician who had been called in, remarking
the disorder of his pulse, asked if his mind was at ease.
" No, it is not," was the reply. These were the last
words he spoke. On the morning of Monday, the 4th
of April, 1774, after a long-hoped-for sleep, he died in
strong convulsions, having lived forty-five years and five
months. The announcement of his death came like a
shock upon his friends. Burke burst into tears ; Sir
Joshua laid aside his pencil for the day ; and a deeper
gloom settled upon Johnson. At Brick Court other, and
humbler mourners, to whom he had been kind, filled the
little staircase with their sorrow ; and, as he lay in his
coffin, a lock of his hair was cut from his head for
the "Jessamy Bride" and her sister.[1] On Saturday the
9th, after some discussion as to a public funeral, which
was abandoned on account of the state of his affairs, he
was buried quietly in the burying-ground of the Temple
Church, none weeping more profusely over his grave
than his old rival, Hugh Kelly. Two years later, a

[1] It is still in the possession of Mrs. Gwyn's descendants.

monument, with a medallion portrait by Nollekens, and an epitaph by Johnson, the story of which must be read in Boswell, was erected to him in Westminster Abbey at the expense of the Literary Club. Johnson's Latin—for he refused to " disgrace " that time-honoured fane by English, ran as follows :—

OLIVARII GOLDSMITH
Poetæ, Physici, Historici,
qui nullum fere scribendi genus
non tetigit,
nullum quod tetigit non ornavit :
sive risus essent movendi,
sive lacrymæ,
affectuum potens, at lenis dominator ;
ingenio sublimis, vividus, versatilis ;
oratione grandis, nitidus, venustus :
hoc monumento memoriam coluit
Sodalium amor,
Amicorum fides,
Lectorum veneratio.
Natus Iiberniâ, Forneiæ Lonfordiensis
in loco cui nomen Pallas
Nov. xxix. MDCCXXXI.
Eblanæ literis institutus,
Objit Londini
Ap. iv. MDCCLXXIV.[1]

---

[1] Croker translates this as follows :—" Of Oliver Goldsmith—a Poet, Naturalist, and Historian, who left scarcely any style of writing untouched, and touched nothing that he did not adorn ; of all the passions, whether smiles were to be moved or tears, a powerful yet gentle master ; in genius, sublime, vivid, versatile ; in style, elevated, clear, elegant—the love of Companions, the fidelity of Friends, and the veneration of Readers, have by this monument honoured the memory. He was born in Ireland, at a place called

The date of birth, it will be seen, is inaccurately given. Many years after this monument had been erected in Westminster, a tablet, now removed to the vestry, was put up in the Temple Church by the Benchers. But the exact spot where Oliver Goldsmith lies is not known, although a flat stone at the north side of the church marks it conjecturally, and is perhaps more piously visited by pilgrims than either of the other memorials. In January, 1864, a full-length statue by Foley, the Academician, was placed in front of Dublin University.[1]

Pallas [in the parish] of Forney, [and county] of Longford, on the 29th November, 1731. Educated at [the University of] Dublin, and died in London, 4th April, 1774."

[1] "Retaliation" (see p. 179) was published on the 19th April, a fortnight after its author's death. In June followed "Animated Nature," and in 1776 "The Haunch of Venison," to the second edition of which were added two songs from "The Captivity," an oratorio written in 1764, but not published as a whole until 1820.

CHAPTER XII.

SOMETHING of Goldsmith's personal appearance will already have been gathered from the foregoing pages, and more particularly from the letter to his brother quoted at the beginning of chapter iv. He was short and stoutly built. His complexion was pale or sallow, and he was deeply scarred by the smallpox. His scant hair was brown, his eyes gray or hazel, and his forehead, which was rather low, projected in a way that is easily exaggerated in some of the copies of his portraits. Yet "his features"—if we may trust one who knew him—though "plain," were "not repulsive,—certainly not so when lighted up by conversation." Another witness, Mrs. Gwyn, says that his countenance bore every trace of his unquestionable benevolence. His true likeness must probably be sought between the slightly grotesque sketch by his friend Bunbury, prefixed to the early editions of "The Haunch of Venison," and the portrait by Reynolds at Knole Park, of which there is a copy in the National Portrait Gallery. Mr. Forster is severe upon Bunbury's "caricature;" but it should be remembered that "The Jessamy Bride" (who, even if prejudiced in favour of her brother-in-law's art, can scarcely be suspected of any desire to depreciate Goldsmith) declares that it "gives the head with admirable fidelity as he actually lived among us." " Nothing (she adds) can exceed its truth." On the other hand, she says of Reynolds's picture, that "it was painted as a fine poetical head for the admiration of posterity," but "was not the man as seen in daily life." This is obviously just. In the noble portrait by Sir Joshua personal regard has idealized the resemblance, and the artist, to use his familiar phrase, has put into his sitter's head something from his own. His finely perceptive genius has fixed for ever the most appealing characteristics of his friend's inner nature, his "exquisite sensibility of contempt," his wistful hunger for recognition, his craving to be well with all men. The only other portrait which needs mention is that prefixed to Evans's edition of the " Poetical and Dramatic Works." It stands (with less individuality) between the other two, and may be a copy of the miniature to which Goldsmith refers in his letter to his brother Maurice, of January, 1770. " I have sent my cousin Jenny a miniature picture of myself, as I believe it is the most acceptable present I can offer. . . . The face you know is ugly enough, but it is finely painted."

The words last quoted might be adduced as evidence that Goldsmith was not always as vain as some of his contemporaries would have us believe. He was, in reality, of so open and unguarded a disposition, and so wholly incapable of any conventional concealment of his thoughts and emotions, that in collecting anecdotes to illustrate his character, it is of the first importance to ascertain whether the narrator is a friend or an enemy.

Side by side with many rare and noble qualities, Goldsmith had many weaknesses, which were sometimes, especially to unsympathetic observers, far more manifest than his merits. " The doctor," says one contemporary, " was a perfect Heteroclite, an inexplicable existence in creation; such a compound of absurdity, envy, and malice, contrasted with the opposite virtues of kindness, generosity, and benevolence, that he might be said to consist of two distinct souls, and influenced by the agency of a good and bad spirit." This was the opinion of Davies the bookseller, who had known him intimately, and could hardly be described as either friend or foe, unless his position as Garrick's biographer puts him *ex officio* in the latter category. But the passage serves to show that Goldsmith was, above all, a man of whom, to echo a Greek idiom, we should " truth it in love," and, in this connection, the testimony of witnesses such as Johnson and Reynolds, or even as Glover and Cooke, is of far greater import than that of Walpole, or Boswell, or Hawkins, who scarcely ever speak of him without an accent of disdain or patronage.

That Goldsmith's last years were one prolonged struggle with embarrassment has been sufficiently asserted. It seems equally clear that his difficulties arose less from lack of means, or inadequate remuneration, than from his constitutional heedlessness. Nor can it be doubted that they played their part in shortening his life. "Of poor dear Dr. Goldsmith "—wrote Johnson to Boswell—" there is little to be told, more than the papers have made publick. He died of a fever, made, I am afraid, more violent by uneasiness of mind. His debts began to be heavy, and all

his resources were exhausted. Sir Joshua is of opinion
that he owed not less than two thousand pounds. Was
ever poet so trusted before?" To Langton, in a letter
bearing the next day's date, the story is the same. "He
[Goldsmith] died of a fever, exasperated, as I believe,
by the fear of distress. He had raised money and
squandered it, by every artifice of acquisition, and folly
of expense. But let not his frailties be remembered;
he was a very great man." These utterances are, in
part, confirmed by the record, incomplete as it must
necessarily be, of the amounts he had received since the
success of "The Good Natur'd Man" in 1768. A
rough calculation of his ascertained gains from that date
gives over £3,000—a sum, in all probability, much
below his actual receipts. If, as Reynolds thought, his
debts came to "not less than £2,000," he must, for the
last six years of his life, have been living at the rate of
at least £800 a year, a sum which, to Johnson, with
the modest pension of £300, out of which he managed
to maintain so many other pensioners of his own, must
have had all "the glitter of affluence." On the other
hand, it should be remembered that Goldsmith's income
was not paid with the regularity of a State stipend.
Yet it was an income which, with moderate care, might
have sufficed for a bachelor. Even if the £2,000 debt
be deducted, there still remains an income of £500, or
£200 more than Johnson's pension, and more than
double the allowance Lord Auchinlech made to Boswell.
To acquit Goldsmith of "folly of expense" is therefore
impossible. It is clear that his money must have "burnt
his pocket" as freely in his later years, as in those

earlier days, when he first set out to study law in London.

Johnson might have saved much speculation if he had thrown some light on the specific prodigalities to which he indirectly refers. Was gambling one of them? If we are to believe Cradock, it was. "The greatest real fault of Dr. Goldsmith," he says, "was, that if he had thirty pounds in his pocket, he would go into certain companies in the country, and in hopes of doubling the sum, would generally return to town without any part of it." Cooke and Davies speak much to the same effect; and the fact that Garrick, in one of his epitaphs, calls him "gamester," may at least be taken to signify that the accusation of play was currently made against him. Moreover, it had been alleged to be one of his especial temptations, even in his younger days, and when he was a student at Leyden. Both Mr. Forster and Mr. Prior, doubtless with praiseworthy intentions, endeavour to palliate this weakness, by proving that Goldsmith could not have "played high;" but to a man with an uncertain income, a trifling loss would be far more disastrous than those easy thousands which Fox and Lord March flung away at the hazard table. Added to this he had apparently but few qualifications for success in this direction. He may have been unlucky at cards, but he was, admittedly, "exceedingly inexpert in their use," as well as impatient of temper.

Another source of extravagance was undoubtedly the succession of splendid garments, in which, with the assistance of Mr. William Filby, at the sign "of the Harrow, in Water Lane," he was wont, in Judge Day's expression, to "exhibit his muscular little person." This had been a frailty from his boyhood — witness the story of the Elphin red breeches, and the Edinburgh student bills. Something of vanity was doubtless mingled with it, but the desire to extenuate his personal short-comings, and the mistaken idea of the importance of fine clothes to the gentleman, had also considerable influence. Certainly, in his better moments, he was fully conscious of the futility of squandering money in this way. Once Reynolds found him in a reverie, kicking a bundle mechanically round the room. Upon examination, this proved to be an expensive masquerade dress, which he had been tempted to purchase, and out of which, its temporary ends having been served, he was endeavouring, as he jestingly said, to extract the value in exercise. At his death he owed Filby £79, although only the previous year he had paid him sums amounting in all to £110. It is but fair to add that £35 of this £79 was incurred for a ne'er-do-well nephew from Ireland, who, when he afterwards became a prosperous "squireen," never thought it due to his uncle's memory to discharge the balance. And nowhere more fitly than in this place can it be recorded that the tailor always spoke well of his dis-tinguished debtor. "He had been a good customer," said honest Mr. Filby of the Harrow; "and had he lived would have paid every farthing." Nor was Mr. Filby the only person who was charitably disposed to that kindly spendthrift at Brick Court. There were two poor Miss Gunns, milliners at the corner of Temple Lane, who told Cradock that they would work for his friend for nothing, rather than that he should go elsewhere. "We are sure

that he will pay us if he can." Such testimonies out-
balance long files of overdue accounts.

His paying the bills of his nephew Hodson explains
another of his methods of spending money, which
perhaps only the most rigid moralists will regard as a
"folly of expense." There can be no doubt of his
hospitality and generosity. His entertainments, when
he was in a position to entertain, and, frequently
when he was not, were of the most lavish character.
Once, when one of his dinners had opened with more
than usual profusion, Johnson and Reynolds, who suspected his pecuniary embarrassments, silently rebuked him
by sending away the second course untouched—a mode
of admonition surely more humiliating than salutary.
As to his benevolence, it may fairly be said to have been
boundless, though unhappily it was often ill-bestowed.
If his benefactions had been confined to the poor women
who carried away the remains of his breakfast on "shoemaker's holidays," or to his landlady in Green Arbour
Court, who, until his death, found in him a faithful friend,
he might have been, if not a rich, at least a solvent man.
But his literary prominence drew about him a host of
parasites and petitioners, mostly from his native island,
who practised upon his kind heart, and his compassionate
impulses. He had learned from his father to be a "mere
machine of pity," and the Purdons and Pilkingtons who
preyed upon him, took care that the machine should not
rust for lack of use. Upon the whole it may be concluded that more of his money went in this way than in
any other. "His humanity and generosity," says Hawes,
"greatly exceeded the narrow limits of his fortune." And

Hawes, as his temporary executor, had special facilities for knowing.

The "envy and malice" with which he is credited by Davies were probably more apparent than real. Nevertheless his recorded attitude to Sterne, Gray, Beattie, Churchill, and others of his contemporaries, shows that he cannot be entirely absolved from hearing

> "in every breeze
> The laurels of Miltiades;"

and there are passages in Boswell, which, although they do not support the charge of malice, can scarcely be disregarded, even when every allowance has been made for bias in the teller. "Talking of Goldsmith," writes Boswell, "Johnson said, he was very envious. I defended him by observing that he owned it frankly upon all occasions. 'Sir' [said Johnson] 'you are enforcing the charge. He had so much envy, that he could not conceal it. He was so full of it that he overflowed. He talked of it to be sure often enough. Now, Sir, what a man avows, he is not ashamed to think, though many a man thinks, what he is ashamed to avow.'" To this may be appended a qualifying passage from Davies: "Goldsmith was so sincere a man, that he could not conceal what was uppermost in his mind. . . His envy was so childish, and so absurd, that it may be very easily pardoned, for everybody laughed at it; and no man was ever very mischievous whose errors excited mirth; he never formed any scheme, or joined in any combination, to hurt

any man living."[1] Closely allied to this uncontrollable
candour of character was a simplicity which was part of
his Irish nature, and which often made him the butt of
his contemporaries. The anecdote of Gibbon's palming
off Montezuma upon him for Porus has already been
related. Another story told by Croker, exhibits him as the
innocent dupe of Burke: "Colonel O'Moore, of Clog-
han Castle in Ireland, told me an amusing instance of
the mingled vanity and simplicity of Goldsmith, which
(though, perhaps, coloured a little as anecdotes too often
are) is characteristic at least of the opinion which his best
friends entertained of Goldsmith. One afternoon, as
Colonel O'Moore and Mr. Burke were walking to dine
with Sir Joshua Reynolds, they observed Goldsmith (also
on his way to Sir Joshua's) standing near a crowd of
people, who were staring and shouting at some foreign
women in the windows of one of the hotels of Leicester
Square. 'Observe Goldsmith,' said Mr. Burke to
O'Moore, 'and mark what passes between him and
me by and by at Sir Joshua's.' They passed on and
arrived before Goldsmith, who came soon after, and Mr.
Burke affected to receive him very coolly. This seemed
to vex poor Goldsmith, who begged Mr. Burke to tell him
how he had had the misfortune to offend him. Burke
appeared very reluctant to speak ; but, after a good deal
of pressing, said that he was really ashamed to keep up

---

[1] Percy writes much to the same effect : "Whatever appeared
of this kind was a mere momentary sensation, which he knew not
how like other men to conceal. It was never the result of principle,
or the suggestion of reflection ; it never imbittered his heart, nor
influenced his conduct."

an intimacy with one who could be guilty of such mon-
strous indiscretions as Goldsmith had just exhibited in
the square." Goldsmith, with great earnestness, protested
he was unconscious of what was meant. 'Why,' said
Burke, 'did you not exclaim, as you were looking up at
those women, what stupid beasts the crowd must be for
staring with such admiration at those 'painted Jezebels!'
while a man of your talents passed by unnoticed?"
Goldsmith was horror-struck, and said, 'Surely, surely,
my dear friend, I did not say so!' 'Nay,' replied Burke,
'if you had not said so, how should I have known it?'
'That's true,' answered Goldsmith, with great humility;
'I am very sorry—it was very foolish; I do recollect that
something of the kind passed through my mind, but I did
not think I had uttered it.'" It is the simplicity rather
than the vanity of Goldsmith which is here illustrated,
and the blame of the story, if any, certainly lies with
Burke.

In attempting to estimate Goldsmith as he struck his
contemporaries—to use Mr. Browning's phrase—it is
important to bear in mind his history and antecedents.
Born a gentleman, he had, nevertheless, started in life with
few temporal or personal advantages, and with a morbid
susceptibility that accentuated his defects. His younger
days had been aimless and unprofitable. Until he became
a middle-aged man, his career had been one of which,
even now, we do not know all the degradations, and
they had left their mark upon his manners. Although
he knew Percy as early as 1759, and Johnson in 1761, it
was not until the establishment of "The Club," or perhaps even until the publication of "The Traveller," that

he became really introduced to society, and he entered it with his past associations still clinging about him. If he was —not unnaturally—elated at his success, he seems also to have displayed a good deal of that nervous self-consciousness, which characterizes those who experience sudden alternations of fortune. To men like Johnson, who had been intimate with him long, and recognized his genius, his attitude presented no difficulty, but to the ordinary spectator he seemed awkward and ill at ease, prompting once more the comment, that genius and knowledge of the world are seldom fellow-lodgers. On his own part, too, he must have been often uncertain of his position and capricious in his demands. Sometimes he was tenacious in the wrong place, and if he thought himself neglected, had not the tact to conceal his annoyance. Once, says Boswell, he complained to a mixed company that, at Lord Clare's, Lord Camden had taken no more notice of him than if he "had been an ordinary man"—an utterance which required all Johnson's championship to defend. At other times he would lament to Reynolds that he seemed to strike a kind of awe upon those into whose company he went, an awe which he endeavoured to dispel by excess of hilarity and sociability. "Sir Joshua," says Northcote (or Laird, who collected Northcote's "Recollections"), "was convinced, that he was intentionally more absurd, in order to lessen himself in social intercourse, trusting that his character would be sufficiently supported by his works." This anecdote may pair off with the story of that affected solemnity by which he sometimes imposed upon those about him; but in either case the part is a dangerous one to play.

As a conversationalist he seems to have had but few qualifications for success. Like Burke he never lost, nor, to the end of his life, cared to lose, his strong Irish accent. He seems besides, as he himself tells us, to have suffered from that most fatal of all drawbacks to a *raconteur*, a slow and hesitating manner; and he was easily disconcerted by retort or discomfited in argument. He reasoned best, he said, with his pen in his hand. These things were all against him, and they were intensified by the competition into which he was thrown. Among ordinary men he might have shone, but his chief associates in later life were some of the most brilliant talkers of his own, or any age. Few could hope to contend on equal terms with the trained dialectics and inexhaustible memory of Johnson, or to rival the mental affluence and brilliant rhetoric of Burke. And besides these, there were the refined scholarship of Langton, the easy *savoir-vivre* of Beauclerk, the wit and mercurial alertness of Garrick. Speaking to Boswell, Johnson seems to have put Goldsmith's position in his usual straightforward manner: "The misfortune of Goldsmith in conversation is this : he goes on without knowing how he is to get off. His genius is great, but his knowledge is small. As they say of a generous man, it is a pity he is not rich, we may say of Goldsmith, it is a pity he is not knowing. He would not keep his knowledge to himself." Again : "Goldsmith should not be for ever attempting to shine in conversation ; he has not temper for it, he is so much mortified when he fails. Sir, a game of jokes is composed partly of skill, partly of chance, a man may be beat at times by one who has not the tenth part of his wit. Now

Goldsmith's putting himself against another, is like a man laying a hundred to one who cannot spare the hundred. It is not worth a man's while. A man should not lay a hundred to one, unless he can easily spare it, though he has a hundred chances for him : he can but get a guinea, and he may lose a hundred. Goldsmith is in this state. When he contends, if he gets the better, it is a very little addition to a man of his literary reputation ; if he does not get the better he is miserably vexed." It is quite possible that these utterances lost nothing under Boswell's recording pen. As a slight corrective to them may be cited a passage from " The Parlour Window " of the Reverend Edward Mangin, who, as far as we are aware, has not hitherto been brought forward as a witness. " I knew an old literary man, a very keen observer too, who assured me that he had often been in company with Goldsmith, Johnson, Garrick, &c., and that Goldsmith used to have a crowd of listeners about his seat, and was a shrewd and eloquent converser." It is also incontestable that, whatever Goldsmith's success may have been in the " wit-combats " at the Turk's Head, he frequently said very pertinent things. Such was his affirmation of Burke, that " he wound into a subject like a serpent ; " such his rebuke to Boswell, babbling of Johnson's supremacy, that he was "for making a monarchy of what should be a republic." Nor was this the only one of his random flashes that went home to the great lexicographer himself. It was Goldsmith who said of Johnson that he had nothing of the bear but the skin; that he would make the little fishes talk like whales; that if his pistol [of argument] missed fire, he knocked you down with the butt end

thereof—all of which bid fair to attain the most advanced
age accorded to fortunate epigrams.

Some of the pleasantest anecdotes of Goldsmith's
career are connected with Johnson. No one seems to
have dared to make that great man " rear " in precisely
the same way as " Doctor *Minor.*" Once, relates Johnson
—in a well-remembered instance—they were in Westminster Abbey together, and pausing in Poets' Corner,
Johnson said, sonorously (as we may assume) :—

" Forsitan et nostrum nomen miscebitur istis. "

As they returned citywards, Goldsmith pointed slyly to
the blanching heads on Temple Bar.

" Forsitan et nostrum nomen miscebitur *istis*,"—

he whispered. On another occasion they were supping
on rumps and kidneys at a tavern. " Sir," said Johnson,
" these rumps are pretty little things ; but then a man
must eat a great many of them before he fills his
belly." " Aye," interjected Goldsmith, "but how many
of these would reach to the moon ? " " To the moon ! "
echoed Johnson ; "that, Sir, I fear, exceeds your calcula-
tions." " Not at all," said Goldsmith, firmly ; " I think
I could tell." " Pray then let us hear." " Why," said
Goldsmith again, speaking deliberately, " *one*, if it were
long enough." Well might Johnson gasp—" Sir, I have
deserved it ; I should not have provoked so foolish an
answer by so foolish a question." But the prettiest inci-

dent of all is perhaps the story of the little quarrel at
Dilly's in the Poultry. Johnson had had a long innings of
talk, and Goldsmith, "burning to get in and shine" (according to Boswell), was afraid, from some uncouth sound the
great man emitted, that he was preparing to start afresh.
" 'Sir (said he to Johnson), the gentleman has heard you
patiently for an hour; pray allow us now to hear him.'
'Sir (retorted Johnson, sternly), I was not interrupting the
gentleman. I was only giving him a signal of my attention. Sir, you are impertinent!' Goldsmith made no
reply, but continued in the company some time." A
little later Boswell takes up the sequel. " He [Johnson]
and Mr. Langton and I went together to the Club, where
we found Mr. Burke, Mr. Garrick, and some other
members, and amongst them our friend Goldsmith, who
sat silently brooding over Johnson's reprimand to him
after dinner. Johnson perceived this, and said aside to
some of us, 'I'll make Goldsmith forgive me,' and then
called to him in a loud voice—' Dr. Goldsmith,—something passed to-day where you and I dined; I ask your
pardon.' Goldsmith answered placidly, 'It must be
much from you, Sir, that I take ill.' And so at once the
difference was over, and they were on as easy terms as
ever, and Goldsmith rattled away as usual." Such differences, indeed, were but momentary. Both men had a
sincere admiration for each other,—an admiration to
which the survivor often testified with a frank fidelity.
Once, not long after Goldsmith's death, when some
busy-bodies at Reynolds's were depreciating his work,
Johnson, we are told, rose with great dignity, looked
them full in the face, and exclaimed, " If nobody was

suffered to abuse poor Goldy but those who could write as well, he would have few censors!" Upon another and later occasion, when he was discussing Goldsmith in his own particularly truthful way, he said to Sir Joshua : " Goldsmith was a man, who, whatever he wrote, did it better than any other man could do. He deserved a place in Westminster Abbey, and every year he lived, would have deserved it better."

But there must come an end to anecdote—even in a brief biography. It would be easy to multiply examples of that strange mingling of strength and weakness—of genius and *gaucherie*—which went to make up Goldsmith's character. Yet the advantage would remain with its gentler and more lovable aspects, and the " over-word " would still be the compassionate verdict : " Let not his frailties be remembered, for he was a very great man." And—what is perhaps more to the purpose of the present series of memoirs—he was assuredly a Great Writer. In the fifteen years over which his literary activity extended, he managed to produce a record which has given him an unassailable position in English letters. Apart from mere hack work and compilation—hack work and compilation which, in most cases, he all but lifted to the level of a fine art—he wrote some of the best familiar verse in the language. In an age barren of poetry, he wrote two didactic poems, which are still among the memories of the old, as they are among the first lessons of the young. He wrote a series of essays, which, for style and individuality, fairly hold their own between the best work of Addison and Steele on the one hand, and the best work of Charles Lamb on the other. He wrote a domestic novel, unique

in kind, and as cosmopolitan as " Robinson Crusoe."
Finally he wrote two excellent plays, one of which,
"She Stoops to Conquer," still stands in the front
rank of the few popular masterpieces of English
comedy.

THE END.

APPENDIX.

S INCE the last line of this book was printed, the
author has been permitted, by the kindness of Mr.
F. Locker-Lampson, to transcribe from his collection
of autographs, and to reproduce—it is believed for the
first time—the following letters of Goldsmith. They
relate to William Hodson, the nephew mentioned at p.
191; and supply fresh examples of his uncle's kindliness
and generosity. The arrangement is conjectural.

[*No date.*]

My DEAR BROTHER,—I have the pleasure of informing you that
your son William is arrived in London in safety and joins with
me in his kindest love and duty to you. Nothing gives me greater
pleasure than the prospect I have of his behaving in the best and
most dutiful manner both to you and the rest of the family. Sincerely
I am charmed with his disposition and I am sure he feels all the
good nature he expresses every moment for his friends at home.
He had when he came here some thoughts of going upon the
stage; I dont know where he could have contracted so beggarly an
affection, but I have turned him from it and he is now sincerely
bent on pursuing the study of physic and surgery in which he has
already made a considerable progress and to which I have very
warmly exhorted him. He will in less than a year be a very good
Surgeon and he will understand a competent share of physic also.

when he is fit for any business or any practice I shall use all my little interest in his favour. As for the stage it was every way a wild scheme and he is beside utterly unfit to succeed upon it. But while he is fitting himself for other business my dear Brother it is not proper that he should be utterly neglected. I have endeavoured to answer for you and my sister that some little thing should be done for him either here or at Edinburgh, and for my own part I am willing to contribute something towards his education myself. I believe an hundred pounds for a year or two would very completely do the business, when once he has got a profession he then may be thrown into any place with a prospect of succeeding. My Dear Dan think of this for a little, something *must* be done. I will give him twenty pounds a year, he has already about twenty more, the rest must be got, and your own good sense will suggest the means. I have often told you and tell you again that we have all good prospects before us, so that a little perseverance will bring things at last to bear. My brother Maurice was with me in London but it was not in my power to serve him effectually then; indeed in a letter I wrote him I desired him by no means to come up but he was probably fond of the journey. I have already written to Dr. Hunter in William's favour, and have got him cloaths, etc. I only wait your answer in what manner further to proceed and with the sincerest affection to you and my sister I am Dear Dan your most affectionate   Brother

OLIVER GOLDSMITH.

I had a letter from Charles who is as he tells me possessed of a competency and settled in Jamaica.

Danl Hodson Esqr.

[*No date.*]

MY DEAR BROTHER,—It gave me great concern to find that you were uneasy at your son's going abroad. I will beg leave to state my part in the affair and I hope you will not condemn me for what I have endeavoured to do for his benefit. When he came here first I learned that his circumstances were very indifferent, and that something was to be done to retrieve them. The stage was an abominable resource which neither became a man of honour, nor a man of sense. I therefore dissuaded him from that design and turned him to physic in which he had before made a very great progress, and since that he has for this last twelve months applied himself to surgery, so that I am thoroughly convinced that there is not a better surgeon in the kingdom of Ireland than he. I was obliged to go down to Bath with a friend that was dying when my nephew sent me down your letter to him in which you inform him that he can no longer have any expectations from you and that therefore he must think of providing for himself. With this letter he sent me one of his own where he asserted his fixed intentions of going surgeon's mate to India. Upon reading the two letters I own I thought something was to be done. I therefore wrote to a friend in Town who procured him the assurance of a place as full surgeon to India. This with supplying him with about five and forty pounds is what I did in my endeavours to serve him. I thought him helpless and unprovided for, and I was ardent in my endeavours to remove his perplexities. Whatever his friends at home may think of a surgeon's place to the East Indies, it is not so contemptible a thing, and those who go seldom fail of making a moderate fortune in two or three voyages. But be this as it may William is now prevailed upon to return home to take your further advice and instructions upon the matter. He has laboured very hard since he left you, and is capable of living like a gentleman in any part of the world. He has answered his examinations as a Surgeon and has been found sufficiently qualified. I entreat therefore you will receive him as becomes him and you, and that you will endeavour to serve the young man effectually not by foolish fond caresses but by either advancing him in his business or setling him in life. I could my Dear Brother say a great deal more, but am obliged to hasten this letter as I am again just setting out for Bath, and I honestly say I had much rather it had been for Ireland with my nephew, but that pleasure I hope to have before I die.

I am Dear Dan
Your most affectionate
Brother OLIVER GOLDSMITH.

Daniel Hodson Esq.

TEMPLE. BRICK COURT.
December 16 1772

DEAR SIR,—I received your letter, inclosing a draft upon Kerr and company which when due shall be applied to the discharge of

a part of my nephew's debts.   He has written to me from Bristol
for ten pound which I have sent him in a bank note enclosed   he
has also drawn upon me by one Mr. Odonogh for ten pound more,
the balance therefore having paid his servant maid, as likewise one
or two trifles more remains with me.   As he will certainly have
immediate and pressing occasion for the rest when he arrives I beg
youl remit the rest to me and I will take care to see it applied in the
most proper manner.   He has talked to me of a matrimonial scheme.
If that could take place all would soon be well.   I am Dear Sir
your affection Kinsman and humble servant

OLIVER GOLDSMITH.

Be pleased to answer this directly
Mr Thomas Bond Attorney
            in Montrath Street
                    Dublin

Little definite is known respecting William Hodson.
He was the son of Daniel Hodson and Catherine, Goldsmith's second sister (*vide* p. 19).   Cradock says he practised as an apothecary in Newman Street ; and it is
further alleged of him that he once paid a small debt
with an undrawn lottery ticket which came up a prize of
£20,000.   In 1807, according to Dr. Strean, his son,
Oliver Goldsmith Hodson, had succeeded to the paternal
estate.   The Dr. Hunter, mentioned at p. 204, is probably
Dr. William Hunter ; and the closing lines of the second
letter (p. 205) tend to confirm the belief that Goldsmith
never re-visited Ireland after he left it in 1752.

INDEX.

⸻

BIBLIOGRAPHY.

BY

JOHN P. ANDERSON

(British Museum).

I. WORKS.

The Miscellaneous Works of Oliver
Goldsmith, containing all his
Essays and Poems. London,
1775, 8vo.

The Miscellaneous Works of O. G.,
now first uniformly collected.
7 vols. Perth, 1792, 8vo.

The Miscellaneous Works of O. G.
A new edition, to which is prefixed some account of his life
and writings [compiled for Bp.
Percy; the whole edited by S.
Rose]. 4 vols. London, 1801.
8vo.

——Another edition. 5 vols.
London, 1806, 12mo.

The Miscellaneous Works of O. G.
A new edition [by S. Rose],
to which is prefixed some
account of his life and writings
[compiled for Bp. Percy]. 4
vols. London, 1812, 8vo.

——Another edition. 4 vols.
London, 1820, 8vo.

The Miscellaneous Works of O. G.
With an account of his life and
writings. A new edition,
edited by Washington Irving.
4 vols. Paris, 1825, 8vo.
    Part of the "Collection of English
Literature."

The Miscellaneous Works of O. G.
A new edition, to which is prefixed some account of his life

and writings. 6 vols. London, 1823, 12mo.

The Miscellaneous Works of O. G., including a variety of pieces now first collected. By James Prior. 4 vols. London, 1837, 8vo.

With engraved title-page also to each volume.

The Miscellaneous Works of O. G., to which is prefixed some account of his life and writings. A new edition, complete in one volume. Edinburgh, 1843, 8vo.

The Works of O. G. Edited by Peter Cunningham. 4 vols. London, 1854, 8vo.

Part of "Murray's British Classics."

——Another edition. 4 vols. London, 1854, 8vo.

The Works of O. G., with introductory memoir by William Spalding. (Facsimile of a letter by O. G., etc.) London, 1858, 8vo.

The Poetical and Prose Works of O. G., with life. Eight engravings on steel. Edinburgh [1859], 8vo.

The Works of O. G., illustrated. Vicar of Wakefield, Select Poems, and Comedies. With introductions, notes, and a life of O. G. by John F. Waller. London, 1864-65, 4to.

The edition issued in 1871-72 is merely a duplicate of this work with a new title-page.

The Miscellaneous Works of O. G., comprising the Vicar of Wakefield, Citizen of the World, Poetical Works, etc., with an account of his life and writings. Edinburgh, 1865, 8vo.

The Complete Works of O. G., comprising his Essays, Poetical Works, and Vicar of Wakefield,

etc. New edition. London, 1867, 8vo.

The Miscellaneous Works of O. G., with biographical introduction by Professor Masson. (*The Globe Edition.*) London, 1869 [1868], 8vo.

The Works of O. G. Illustrated by F. Gilbert. London, 1869, 8vo.

The Complete Works of O. G., comprising his Essays, Plays, and Poetical Works. With a memoir by William Spalding. New edition. (*Blackwood's Universal Library of Standard Authors*). London [1872], 8vo.

The Poetical and Prose Works of O. G., with life. Engravings on steel. (*Landscape Series of Poets.*) Edinburgh [1881], 8vo.

The Works of O. G. A new edition, containing pieces hitherto uncollected, and a life of the author. With notes from various sources by J. W. M. Gibbs. (*Bohn's Standard Library.*) 5 vols. London, 1834-6, 8vo.

II. SMALLER COLLECTIONS.

Poems and Plays by O. G. To which is prefixed the life of the author. Dublin, 1777, 8vo.

The Life is a slightly varied issue of the "Anecdotes of the late Dr. Goldsmith" which appeared in the *Annual Register*, 1774, pp. 29-34, signed G.—*i.e.*, Glover.

The Poetical and Dramatic Works of O. G., now first collected. With an account of the life and writings of the author. 2 vols. London, 1780, 8vo.

Another edition. 2 vols. London, 1786, 8vo.

Poems and Plays by O. G., to which is prefixed the life of the author. A new edition, corrected. Dublin, 1785, 12mo.

The Vicar of Wakefield and the Deserted Village. A new edition. London, 1797, 12mo.

The Vicar of Wakefield, with the life of the author, and poem of the Deserted Village. New edition. Birmingham, 1811, 8vo.

Goldsmith's Vicar of Wakefield, Essays, and Poems. With prefatory remarks by John M'Diarmid. Edinburgh, 1823, 12mo.

Essays, Poems, and Plays; with a memoir of the author. London, 1826, 12mo.

The Select Works of O. G., in one volume. (*Tauchnitz Collection of British Authors*, vol. xxii.) Leipzig, 1842, 12mo.

The Vicar of Wakefield and Select Poems. London, 1848, 16mo. In phonetic characters.

The Vicar of Wakefield, together with the poems of O. G. London, 1852, 8vo.

Poems and Vicar of Wakefield. Illustrated by engravings on wood. London [1854], 16mo.

Poems, Plays, and Essays. With a critical dissertation on his poetry, by John Aikin; and an introductory essay by Henry T. Tuckerman. Boston [U.S.], 1854, 12mo.

The Poems and Plays of O. G., with a biographical memoir of the author. (*The Universal Library. Poetry*, vol. ii.) London [1854], 8vo.

The Vicar of Wakefield, and the Deserted Village. Illustrated. London, 1863, 16mo.

The Poetical Works of James Beattie, and the poems and plays of O. G. Edinburgh, [1864], 8vo.

The Poetical Works of James Beattie and the Poems and Plays of O. G. Edinburgh [1865], 8vo.

The Vicar of Wakefield, Poems, and Essays. Edinburgh, [1865], 12mo.

The Vicar of Wakefield, Poems, and Essays. Edinburgh [1868], 8vo.

Goldsmith's Choice Works, comprising his Vicar of Wakefield, Poems, and Plays. (Life of O. G., by T. Finlayson.) Edinburgh, 1871, 8vo.

The Deserted Village; The Traveller; She Stoops to Conquer. Torino, 1872, 8vo.

The Poetical Works, Essays, and the Vicar of Wakefield. With introductory memoir by Professor Spalding. Illustrated. London [1874], 8vo.

The Poems and Plays of O. G. With the addition of the Vicar of Wakefield, memoir, etc. (*Chandos Classics*.) London [1876], 8vo.

The Vicar of Wakefield and other works. With introductions, notes, and a life of O. G., by John F. Waller. London [1877], 4to.

Dramatic Works of Sheridan and Goldsmith. With Goldsmith's Poems. 2 vols. London, 1884, 32mo.

The Vicar of Wakefield and other works [*i.e.*, Miscellaneous Poems and Comedies]. With introductions, notes, and a life, by J. F. Waller. [With illustrations.] London [1885], 8vo.

The Vicar of Wakefield, Plays, and Poems. With an introduction by Henry Morley. (*Morley's Universal Library.*) London, 1885, 8vo.

III. POETICAL WORKS.

The Poetical Works of O. G., complete in one volume. A new edition. London, 1788, 12mo.

Poems. (*Johnson's Works of the English Poets*, vol. lxx.) London, 1790, 8vo.

The Poetical Works of O. G., with an account of the life and writings of the author. A new edition. London, 1793, 8vo.

Poems by Goldsmith [viz., "The Traveller" and "The Deserted Village"] and Parnell [viz., "The Hermit"]. [With woodcuts by T. and J. Bewick.] London, 1795, 4to.
The British Museum possesses a copy on vellum.

The Poetical Works of O. G. (*Anderson's complete edition of the Poets of Great Britain*, vol. x.) London, 1794, 8vo.

The Poetical Works of O. G., complete in one volume. With the life of the author. Embellished with vignettes and tail-pieces, designed and engraved on wood, by T. Bewick. Hereford, 1795, 8vo.

The Poetical Works of O. G., complete in one volume. With the life of the author. Cheltenham, 1798, 8vo.

The Poems of O. G. A new edition. Adorned with plates. London, 1800, 8vo.

The Poetical Works of O. G., with the life of the author. Paris, 1803, 12mo.

Poems [viz., "The Traveller" and "The Deserted Village"] by Goldsmith, and "The Hermit" by Parnell. [Illustrated with woodcuts by T. and J. Bewick.] London, 1804, 8vo.

The Poetical Works, complete, of O. G., with some account of his life and literature. An improved edition, embellished with engravings on wood, by Austin. London, 1804, 8vo.

The Poetical Works of O.G., with a sketch of the author's life; including original anecdotes communicated by the Rev. John Evans. Illustrated, etc. London, 1804, 8vo.

The Poetical Works of O. G., with an account of his life and writings; to which is added a critical dissertation on his poetry, by J. Aikin. London, 1805, 12mo.

The Pleasures of Memory, by Samuel Rogers [and the Poetical Works of O. G., etc.]. Paris, 1805, 12mo.

The Poetical Works of O. G. (*Park's Works of the British Poets*, vol. xxxvii.) London, 1808, 16mo.

The Poetical Works of O. G., with the life of the author. Embellished with woodcuts, by T. Bewick. Glocester, 1809, 12mo.

The Poetical Works of O. G. London [1810], 12mo.

The Poems of Dr. O. G. (*Chambers' English Poets*, vol. xvi.) London, 1810, 8vo.

The Poetical Works of O. G., with remarks, attempting to ascertain chiefly from local observation the actual scene of the Deserted Village; and illustrative engravings by Mr.

Alkin (Alken). By Rev. R. H. Newell. London, 1811, 4to.

The Poetical Works of O. G. Alnwick, 1812, 12mo.

The Traveller and the Deserted Village and other poems. [With engravings from the designs of R. Westall.] London, 1816, 12mo.

The Poetical Works, complete, of O. G., with some account of his life and literature. An improved edition, embellished with engravings on wood, by Austin. London, 1816, 8vo.

The Poetical Works of O. G., with an account of the life and writings of the author. (*The Selector.*) London, 1818, 24mo.

The Poetical Works of O. G., with a sketch of his life. London, 1818, 16mo.

The Poetical Works of O. G., with remarks, attempting to ascertain chiefly from local observation the actual scene of the Deserted Village; and illustrative engravings by Mr. Alkin (Alken). By the Rev. R. H. Newell. London, 1820, 4to.

The Poems of O. G. (*The British Poets*, vol. lxiv.) Chiswick, 1822, 12mo.

Select Poems of O. G., with a life of the author, by Thomas Campbell. (*Works of the British Poets, ed. Walsh*, vol. xxx.) Philadelphia, 1822, 12mo.

The Poetical Works of O. G., with a sketch of his life and writings. [Illustrated.] Chiswick, 1822, 16mo.

The Poetical Works of O. G., with a biographical sketch of the author. London, 1824, 32mo.
Part of "Jones's Diamond Poets."

The Traveller, the Deserted Village, and other poems. [With engravings from th designs of R. Westall.] London, 1826, 12mo.

The Poetical Works of O. G. Life by Rev. J. Mitford. (*Aldine Edition of the British Poets*, vol. xvi.) London, 1831, 8vo.

Poetical Works; edited by B. Corney. With a biographical memoir and notes. London, 1846, 4to.

The Poetical Works of O. G. (*Cabinet Edition of the British Poets*, vol. i.) London, 1851, 8vo.

The Poetical Works of O. G. With thirty illustrations by John Absolon, Birket Foster, etc. London, 1851, 8vo.

The Poetical Works of Oliver Goldsmith, Tobias Smollett, etc. With biographical notices and notes. Illustrated by John Gilbert. (*Routledge's British Poets.*) London, 1853, 8vo.

The Poetical Works of Goldsmith, Beattie, and Campbell. London, 1853, 12mo.

The Poetical Works of Goldsmith, Collins, and T. Warton. With lives, critical dissertations, and explanatory notes, by the Rev. George Gilfillan. Edinburgh, 1854, 8vo.
Part of the "Library edition of the British Poets."

The Poetical Works of O. G., etc. London, 1855, 32mo.

The Poetical Works of Thomson, Goldsmith, and Gray. London, 1855, 8vo.

The Poetical Works of O. G., with a life, by Thomas Babington Macaulay. Boston [U. S.], 1857, 8vo.
The life is reprinted from the *Encyclopædia Britannica.*

The Poetical Works of O. G., with a life by Thomas Babington Macaulay. Boston [U. S.], 1862, 8vo.

This is a duplicate of the preceding, with a new title-page and a new advertisement.

Poetical Works, with life by E. F. Blanchard; illustrated by Birket Foster and others. London, 1858, 8vo.

The Poems of O. G. Edited by Robert Aris Willmott. New edition, with illustrations by Birket Foster and H. N. Humphreys. London, 1859, 4to.

——Another edition. London, 1860, 4to.

The Poetical Works of O. G. With a memoir by William Spalding. [Illustrated.] London, 1864, 8vo.

Dalziels' Illustrated Goldsmith; and a sketch of the life of O. G., by H. W. Dulcken. With one hundred pictures drawn by G. J. Pinwell, engraved by the brothers Dalziel. London, 1865, 4to.

The Poetical Works of O. G.; with a memoir, by William Spalding. Illustrated. London, 1866, 4to.

The Poetical Works of O. G. (The life of O. G., by J. Mitford.) (*Aldine Edition of the British Poets.*) London, 1866, 8vo.

The Poetical Works of O. G., with a notice of his life and genius, by E. F. Blanchard. Illustrated by Birket Foster, etc. London [1867], 8vo.

The Poetical Works of O. G. Illustrated by C. W. Cope, etc. With a biographical memoir. Edited by Bolton Corney. London [1868], 8vo.

Goldsmith. The Traveller, The Deserted Village, and Retaliation. With notes by the Rev. A. R. Vardy. London, 1872, 16mo.

Goldsmith's Traveller and Deserted Village, etc. London [1873], 16mo.

The Traveller and the Deserted Village. With notes, philological and explanatory, by J. W. Hales. London, 1874, 8vo.

Goldsmith's Traveller and the Deserted Village, with introduction, life of the author, argument, and notes, by C. Sankey. (*English School-Classics, ed. F. Storr.*) London, 1874, 16mo.

The Poetical Works of Goldsmith, Collins, and T. Warton. With lives, critical dissertations, and explanatory notes by the Rev. George Gilfillan. The text edited by Charles Cowden Clarke. London [1874], 8vo.

Part of "Cassell's Library Edition of British Poets."

The Deserted Village, and The Traveller. Illustrated. Boston [U. S.], 1876, 24mo.

Part of the "Vest-Pocket Series of Standard and Popular Authors."

The Poetical Works of O. G., Tobias Smollett, Samuel Johnson, etc. With biographical notices, and notes. (*Excelsior Series.*) London [1881], 8vo.

Goldsmith. Selected Poems. Edited, with introduction and notes, by Austin Dobson. (*Clarendon Press Series.*) Oxford, 1887, 8vo.

———

The Captivity; an Oratorio. London, 1836, 12mo.

"This Oratorio was never published by the author." It was first printed in the Trade edition of Goldsmith's Works in 1820.

The Deserted Village, a poem. London, 1770, 4to.

——Second edition. London, 1770, 4to.

——Second edition. Dublin, 1770, 12mo.

——Third edition. London, 1770, 4to.

——Fourth edition. London, 1770, 4to.

——Fifth edition. London, 1770, 4to.

——Sixth edition. London, 1770, 4to.

——Seventh edition. London, 1772, 4to.

——Eighth edition. London, 1775, 4to.

——Ninth edition. London, 1779, 4to.

——The Deserted Village. (*Four Poems,* No. iii.) Altenburgh, 1773, 8vo.

——The Deserted Village. (*A Collection of Poems,* vol. i.) Paris, 1779, 12mo.

——Another edition. London [1780], 8vo.

——Another edition. London [1780], 12mo.

——Another edition. Illustrated by the Etching Club. London, 1841, fol.

——Another edition. Illustrated by the Etching Club. London, 1855, 8vo.

——Goldsmith's Deserted Village, with notes, critical, explanatory, etc., and a life of the poet. By Walter M'Leod. London, 1858, 12mo.

——Second edition. London, 1858, 12mo.

——Another edition. Illustrated

by the Etching Club. London [1875], 8vo.
  Part of "The Choice Series."

——(*Annotated Poems of English Authors, ed. Stevens and Morris.*) London, 1876, 16mo.

——(*Lines from the Poets,* No. iii.) London, 1879, 16mo.

——The Deserted Village. Sketched by F. S. Walker. London [1884], 8vo.

——The Deserted Village. Illustrated. London, 1885, 8vo.

Edwin and Angelina. Privately printed [1765].
  A copy was sold at Heber's sale for 3s. See Prior's Life of Goldsmith, 1837.

The Haunch of Venison, a poetical epistle to Lord Clare. With a head of the author, drawn by Henry Bunbury and etched by Bretherton. London, 1776, 4to.

——Another edition, with considerable additions and corrections, taken from the author's last transcript. London, 1776, 4to.

Retaliation, a Poem; including epitaphs on the most distinguished wits of this metropolis. London, 1774, 4to.

——New edition, with explanatory notes, observations, etc. London, 1774, 4to.

——Third edition, corrected. London, 1774, 4to.

——[Fourth edition,] etc. London, 1774, 4to.

——Fifth edition, corrected. With explanatory notes and observations. London, 1774, 4to.
  This edition contains for the first time the postscript and epitaph on Caleb Whitefoord.

——Eighth edition, with large additions. . . . To which is

added some account of his life. With explanatory notes and observations. London, 1776, 4to.

Mr. Austin Dobson, who possesses a copy, believes it to be unique, or nearly so. The eighth edition, dated 1777, contains The Haunch of Venison, etc. This only contains:—Retaliation; The Hermit; The Gift; Epilogue to the Sisters [Sister]; Epilogue to She Stoops to Conquer; Essay on Friendship; Sabinus and Olinda; Epitaph on Mrs. Mary Blaize. The Life is a slightly varied issue of the "Anecdotes of the late Dr. Goldsmith" which appeared in the *Annual Register*, 1774, pp. 29-34, signed G.—*i.e.*, Glover.

——Eighth edition, with large additions, particularly the Hermit, the Haunch of Venison, and several other pieces by the same author, to which is added some account of his life; with notes, etc. [and an etching of the author from a drawing by Bunbury]. London, 1777, 4to.

——(*The British Satirist*). London, 1826, 12mo.

Threnodia Augustalis; sacred to the memory of Her Royal Highness the Princess Dowager of Wales. London, 1772, 4to.

The Traveller; or, a Prospect of Society. A poem. Inscribed to the Rev. Mr. H. Goldsmith. [First edition.] London, 1765, 4to.

——Second edition. London, 1765, 4to.

——Third edition. London, 1765, 4to.

——Fourth edition. London, 1765, 4to.

——Fifth edition. London, 1768, 4to.

——[Sixth] edition. London, 1770, 4to.

——(*Four Poems*, No. iv.). Altenburgh, 1773, 8vo.

The Traveller. Ninth edition. London, 1774, 4to.

——[Tenth edition]. London, 1778, 4to.

——Another edition. Dublin [1780], 4to.

——Another edition. London [1780], 8vo.

——(*A Collection of Poems*, vol. i.) Paris, 1779, 12mo.

——Another edition. Edinburgh, 1782, 12mo.

——Another edition. Illustrated with etchings on steel by Birket Foster. London [1856], 8vo.

——Another edition. London [1859], 12mo.

——Another edition. With notes, and a brief sketch of the life of Goldsmith by C. P. Mason, etc. London, 1864, 8vo.

——Another edition. With explanatory notes, etc., by W. McLeod. London, 1865, 12mo.

——(*Annotated Poems of English Authors, ed. Stevens and Morris.*) London, 1876, 16mo.

——(*Lines from the Poets*, No. ii.) London, 1879, 16mo.

IV. PROSE WORKS.

Asem, the Man-Hater; an Eastern Tale. With an editorial introduction and illustrations. London, 1877, 4to.

Appeared originally in the volume of *Essays*, 1765.

The Bee. Being Essays on the most interesting subjects. Nos. 1-8. London, 1759, 12mo.

This was a weekly periodical, and ran for eight weeks only, from Oct. 6th to Nov. 24th, 1759. The eight numbers were issued as above in December 1759.

——Another edition. London, 1819, 12mo.

The Citizen of the World; or, Letters from a Chinese Philosopher, residing in London, to his friends in the East. [By O. G.] 2 vols. London, 1762, 12mo.
  Appeared originally in the *Public Ledger* of 1760, 1761.
——Another edition. 2 vols. Dublin, 1769, 12mo.
——Third edition. 2 vols. London, 1774, 8vo.
——Another edition. 2 vols. London, 1792, 12mo.
——(*Harrison's British Classicks*, vol. vi.) London, 1793, 8vo.
——Cooke's edition. 2 vols. London, 1799, 12mo.
  Each volume has also an engraved title-page.
——Another edition. 2 vols. London, 1809, 12mo.
——Another edition. 2 vols. London, 1824, 12mo.
——(*Lynam's British Essayists*, vol. xxi.) London, 1827, 8vo.
——A new edition, with original notes and illustrative woodcuts. London, 1840, 8vo.
——(*The Universal Library*, vol. i.). London, 1854, 8vo.

An Enquiry into the present state of polite learning in Europe. [By O. G.] London, 1759, 8vo.
——Second edition, revised and corrected. London, 1774, 8vo.

Essays. By Mr. Goldsmith. London, 1765, 8vo.
——Second edition, corrected. London, 1766, 12mo.
——Another edition. London, 1775, 8vo.
——Cooke's edition. London, 1799, 12mo.
——Another edition. London, 1819, 12mo.

Essays. (*Lynam's British Essayists*, vol. xxi.) London, 1827, 12mo.
——Another edition. London, 1836, 16mo.
—— (*The Universal Library. Essays*, vol. i.) London, 1853, 8vo.
——Another edition. Selected and edited, with introduction and notes, by C. D. Yonge. London, 1882, 8vo.
——Goldsmith: Selected Essays. Edited, with introduction and notes, by G. Y. Dixon. (*Intermediate Education Series.*) Dublin, 1882, 8vo.

The Grecian History, from the earliest state to the death of Alexander the Great. 2 vols. London, 1774, 8vo.
  Numerous editions. It has been abridged for the use of schools.

An History of the Earth and Animated Nature. [With plates.] 8 vols. London, 1774, 8vo.
——Second edition. 8 vols. London, 1779, 8vo.
  Numerous other editions.
——An Abridgment of Dr. G's Natural History of Beasts and Birds, etc. London, 1807, 12mo.
  Numerous editions.

A History of England in a series of Letters from a nobleman to his son. [By O. G.] 2 vols. London, 1764, 12mo.

The History of England, from the earliest times to the death of George II. 4 vols. London, 1771, 8vo.
  Numerous editions.
—— An Abridgment of the History of England, etc. London, 1774, 12mo.
  Numerous editions.

The Life of Henry St. John, Lord Viscount Bolingbroke [by O. G.]. London, 1770, 8vo.
  Originally prefixed to an edition of Bolingbroke's "Dissertation on Parties," published in 1770.

The Life of Richard Nash, of Bath, Esquire, extracted principally from his original papers. [By O. G.] London, 1762, 8vo.

——Second edition. London, 1762, 8vo.

——Another edition. Dublin, 1762, 12mo.

Poems written by Dr. Thomas Parnell; to which is prefixed The Life of Dr. Parnell, written by Dr. Goldsmith. London, 1770, 8vo.

The Life of Thomas Parnell, compiled from original papers and memoirs : in which are included several letters of Mr. Pope, Mr. Gay, Dr. Arbuthnot, etc. London, 1770, 8vo.

The Martial Review ; or, a general history of the late wars ; together with the Definitive Treaty, and some reflections on the probable consequences of the Peace. [By O. G.] London, 1763, 12mo.

The Mystery Revealed ; containing a series of transactions and authentic testimonials respecting the supposed Cock-Lane Ghost. [By O. G.] London, 1742 [1762], 8vo.

The Roman History, from the foundation of the City of Rome to the destruction of the Western Empire. 2 vols. London, 1769, 8vo.

——Second edition. 2 vols. London, 1770, 8vo.

——Third edition. 2 vols. London, 1775, 8vo.

The Roman History, etc. Fourth edition. 2 vols. London, 1781, 8vo.
  Numerous other editions.

——Dr. Goldsmith's Roman History, abridged by himself for the use of schools. London, 1772, 12mo.
  Numerous editions.

A Survey of Experimental Philosophy considered in its present state of improvement. With cuts. 2 vols. London, 1776, 8vo.

The Vicar of Wakefield : a tale. Supposed to be written by himself. 2 vols. Salisbury, printed by B. Collins for F. Newbery, London, 1766, 12mo.

——The Vicar of Wakefield : a tale. Supposed to be written by himself. 2 vols. London, 1766, 12mo.
  This is an unauthorised reprint of the first edition published for the proprietors by Francis Newbery, March 27, 1766.

——The Vicar of Wakefield : a tale. Supposed to be written by himself. 2 vols. Dublin, 1766, 12mo.
  An unauthorised reprint of the first edition.

——The Vicar of Wakefield : a tale. Supposed to be written by himself. The second edition. 2 vols. London, 1766, 12mo.

——Third edition. 2 vols. London, 1766, 12mo.

——Another edition. 2 vols. Dublin, 1767, 12mo.

——Fourth edition. 2 vols. London, 1770, 12mo.

——Fifth edition. 2 vols. London, 1773, [1774,] 12mo.

——Another edition. Berlin, 1776, 12mo,

——Another edition. 2 vols. London, 1777, 12mo.

The Vicar of Wakefield. Sixth edition. London, 1779.

——Another edition. 2 vols. London, 1780, 12mo.

——Another edition. 2 vols. London, 1781, 8vo.

——Another edition. 2 vols. London, 1781, 12mo.

——First [German] edition. With accents. Halle, 1787, 8vo.

——Eighth edition. [With vignette of the author after Reynolds.] London, 1787, 8vo.

——New edition. [With a frontispiece-portrait entitled "Vicar."] 2 vols. London, 1790, 12mo.

——Another edition. [With plates after Stothard's designs.] London, 1792, 8vo.

—— Twenty-second edition. 2 vols. London, 1792, 12mo.

——Another edition. 2 vols. London [1793], 12mo.
Vol. v. of "Cooke's Edition of Select British Novels."

——Another edition. Embellished with woodcuts by T. Bewick. Hereford, 1798. 8vo.

——Another edition. Vienna, 1798.

——(*Mirror of Amusement*), Liverpool [1800 ?], 8vo.
With plates and engraved title-page.

——Another edition. [With 5 plates designed by Corbould.] London, 1800, 8vo.

——Another edition. Paris [1800,] 12mo.

——Another edition. [With woodcuts.] ——, 1806, 12mo.

——Another edition. [With four full-page woodcuts by A. Anderson.] 2 vols. New York, 1807, 12mo.

——Another edition. [With a copperplate frontispiece by Fairman, and four woodcuts by A. Anderson.] 2 vols. Philadelphia, 1809, 12mo.

——Another edition. [With short sketch of the author, and frontispiece by T. Bewick.] Edinburgh, 1810, 32mo.

——Another edition. [With copper plate frontispiece by Fairman, and four woodcuts by A. Anderson.] Philadelphia, 1810, 24mo.

——(*British Novelists*, vol. xxiii.) London, 1810, 12mo.

——Another edition. To which is prefixed the author's life; including original anecdotes, contributed by J. Evans. [Plates and woodcuts by Craig and Clennell.] London [1812], 8vo.

——Another edition. [With frontispiece by T. Bewick.] Alnwick, 1812, 12mo.

——Another edition. London, 1812, 12mo.
With an engraved title-page and frontispiece. Part of "Walker's British Classics."

——Whittingham's edition. [With woodcuts engraved by John Thompson.] London, 1815, 8vo.

——Another edition. Illustrated with twenty-four designs by Thomas Rowlandson. London, 1817, 8vo.

——Another edition. [With memoirs of O. G., and steel frontispiece drawn by Craig, engraved by Lacey.] London, 1818, 12mo.

——Another edition. With engravings from the designs of R. Westall. London, 1818, 12mo.
There is an engraved title-page with the date 1819. The plates bear also the same date.

The Vicar of Wakefield. Another
edition.] With memoir of the
author by Sir W. Scott.]
(*Novelists' Library*, vol. 5.)
London, 1823, 8vo.

——Another edition, with critical
remarks, and a memoir of the
author. (*British Novelist.*)
London, 1823, 8vo.

——Another edition. Illustrated
with twenty-four designs by T.
Rowlandson. London, 1823,
8vo.

——Another edition. [Illus-
trated with engravings by W.
Finden from designs by R.
Westall.] London, 1828, 16mo.
There is an engraved title with
the date 1829.

——Another edition; with illustrations by George Cruikshank.
(*Roscoe's Novelists' Library*, vol.
x.) London, 1832, 8vo.

——(*Standard Library* edition.
London, 1838, 8vo.

——Another edition, with a prefatory memoir of the author
and his writings. Edinburgh,
1838, 8vo.

——Another edition. New York,
1841, 32mo.

——Another edition. [With 200
woodcuts by G. Dorrington.]
London, 1841, 8vo.
Mentioned by Lowndes.

——Another edition. With illustrations by W. Mulready. London, 1843, 8vo.

——Another edition. Illustrated with 200 wood engravings
and a portrait of the author;
with a prefatory memoir by
G. Moir Bussey. ——, 1844,
8vo.

——Another edition. Printed in
phonography. London, 1848,
12mo.

——(*Illustrated Literature of all

Nations, No. 4.) London [1851],
4to.

——Another edition. Accom-
panied by the life of the author.
London, 1851, 18mo.

——(*Classics Tales.*) London,
1852, 8vo.

——(*The Universal Library.
Fiction*, vol. i.) London,
1853, 8vo.

——The Vicar of Wakefield.
(*Standard Novels.*) London
[1853], 8vo.

——Another edition. London,
1854, 8vo.

——Another edition. London,
1855, 8vo.

——Another edition. Illustrated
by G. Thomas. London, 1855,
8vo.

——Another edition. With illustrations by J. Absolon. London, 1855, 8vo.

——Another edition. With illustrations by Gilbert, Kenny
Meadows, etc. London [1855],
16mo.

——Another edition. London,
1855, 32mo.

——Another edition. London,
1858, 32mo.
One of the "Miniature Classical
Library.'

——Another edition. Illustrated
with numerous engravings.
London [1858], 8vo.

——Another edition. With a
prefatory memoir of the author
and his writings. London,
1859, 16mo.

——Another edition. [With
illustrations.] London [1860],
8vo.

——Another edition. New York
1863.

The Vicar of Wakefield. Another edition. London, 1864, 18mo.
One of Laurie's "Entertaining Library."

——Another edition. New York, 1865, 24mo.

——Another edition. Philadelphia, 1869, 16mo.

——Another edition. With illustrations printed in Oil Colours (Kronheims.) London, 1871, 8vo.

——Another edition. (Life of O. G. by T. Finlayson.) Edinburgh, 1871, 12mo.

——Another edition. [With coloured illustrations.] London [1872], 8vo.

——(*Library of Famous Fiction.*) New York, 1873, 8vo.

——Another edition. Philadelphia, 1874, 12mo.
One of the *Entertaining Library Series.*

——Another edition. Illustrated by G. Thomas. London [1875], 8vo.
Part of "The Choice Series."

——Another edition. Illustrated with twelve fine steel engravings by Sangster. London, 1875, 4to.

——Another edition. New York, 1876, 16mo.
One of the *Riverside Classics.*

——Another edition. Printed in phonography. London [1876], 16mo.

——Another edition. With illustrations. London, 1876, 8vo.

——Another edition. Boston [U.S.], 1877, 18mo.
One of the *Little Classic Edition.*

——Another edition. With a memoir of the author. London, [1878], 8vo.
One of the " Notable Novels."

The Vicar of Wakefield. Another edition. New York, 1879, 32mo.
One of the *Half-Hour Series.*

——Another edition. With illustrations in permanent photography. London, 1880, 8vo.

——Another edition, illustrated. Philadelphia, 1881, 12mo.

——Another edition. With illustrations. London [1882], 8vo.

——The Vicar of Wakefield [by O. G.], Rasselas, (by S. Johnson), Paul and Virginia (by Bernardin de St. Pierre.) With illustrations. 3 parts. London, [1882], 8vo.

——The Vicar of Wakefield. (*Classic Tales* in *Bohn's Standard Library.* London, 1882, 8vo.

——Another edition. With illustrations [1883], 8vo.

——Another edition. With a memoir of Goldsmith by Professor Masson. (*Globe Readings from Standard Authors.*) London, 1883, 8vo.

——Another edition. With a preface and notes by Austin Dobson. (*Parchment Library.*) London, 1883, 8vo.
There were 50 copies printed on large paper. The later issues are slightly revised.

——Another edition. Edinburgh [1884], 8vo.

——The Vicar of Wakefield. (*Blackwood's Educational Series.*) London [1884], 8vo.

——Another edition. Liverpool, 1884.
This edition was issued by the Bon Marché in Barnett Street, Liverpool, at the price of one penny.

——The Vicar of Wakefield. Being a facsimile reproduction of the first edition published in 1766. With an introduction by

Austin Dobson, and a biblio-
graphical list of editions of
"The Vicar of Wakefield" published in England and abroad.
London, 1885, 12mo.

——The Vicar of Wakefield. [In-
troduction by G. T. Bettany.]
(*Routledge's Pocket Library*, vol.
viii.) London, 1886, 16mo.

——Another edition. With prefatory memoir by G. Saintsbury,
and one hundred and fourteen
coloured illustrations [by V. A.
Poirson]. London, 1886, 8vo.

—— ——Goldsmith's Vicar of
Wakefield employed as a means
of reading made easy without
any alteration of orthography.
By C. T. von Kersten. London,
1857, 8vo.

—— ——The Vicar of Wakefield.
Abridged, etc. London, 1883,
8vo.

—— ——Extracts from Gold-
smith's Vicar of Wakefield, with
life of the author, introduction,
connecting narrative, and notes,
by C. Sankey. (*English School
Classics, ed. F. Storr.*) London, 1876, 16mo.

V. DRAMATIC WORKS.

Goldsmith's Plays. Edited by H.
Littledale. (*Blackie's School
Classics.*) London [1884], 8vo.
She Stoops to Conquer, and the
Good-Natured Man. [Edited
by H. Morley.] (*Cassell's Na-
tional Library.*) London, 1886,
8vo.

————

The Good-Natur'd Man; a Comedy
as performed at the Theatre
Royal in Covent Garden. London, 1768, 8vo.

The Good-Natur'd Man. Another
edition. London, 1768, 8vo.
——Fifth edition. London, 1768,
8vo.
——Another edition. Dublin,
1784, 12mo.
——(*Bell's British Theatre*, vol.
xvii.) London, 1797, 8vo.
——Another edition. London,
1807, 8vo.
——(*Inchbald's British Theatre*,
vol. xvii.) London, 1808, 12mo.
——(*Modern British Drama*, vol.
iv.) London, 1811, 8vo.
——(*Dibdin's London Theatre*, vol.
xix.] London. 1816, 16mo.
——(*The London Stage*, vol. ii.)
London [1824], 8vo.
——*Cumberland's British Theatre.*
vol. xiii.) London [1828], 12mo.
——(*Köhler and Seitz's English
Stage*, pt. i.) Jever, 1866, 8vo.
——(*Lacy's Acting Edition of
Plays*, etc., vol. cix) London
[1878], 12mo.
She Stoops to Conquer ; or, the
Mistakes of a Night. A comedy
[in five acts and in prose].
London, 1773, 8vo.
——Another edition. Dublin,
1773, 12mo.
——Fifth edition. London, 1773,
8vo.
—— The Mistakes of a Night, a
Comedy. [She Stoops to Con-
quer.] (*A Collection of New
Plays*, vol. i.) London, 1774,
8vo.
——New edition. London, 1775,
8vo.
——Another edition. London,
1783, 8vo.
——(*Bell's British Theatre*, vol.
ix.) London, 1797, 8vo.
——(*Inchbald's British Theatre.*
vol. xvii.) London [1808], 12mo.

She Stoops to Conquer. (*Modern British Drama*, vol. iv.) London, 1811, 8vo.

—— The Mistakes of a Night [She Stoops to Conquer]. (*Collection of English Plays, with explanatory notes in Danish by F. Schneider*, vol. ii.) Copenhagen, 1812, 12mo.

——(*Dibdin's London Theatre*, vol. vi.) London, 1814, 16mo.

——(*Oxberry's New English Drama*, vol. iv. London, 1818, 8vo.

——She Stoops to Conquer, or the Mistakes of a Night. A Comedy in five acts [and in prose]. (The Fair Penitent. A tragedy by N. Rowe.—The Apprentice. A farce by A. Murphy.—Fortune's Frolic. A farce by J. T. Allingham. 4 pts.) New York, 1824, 16mo.

——(*The London Stage*, vol. i.) London [1824], 8vo.

——(*British Drama*, vol. i.) London, 1824, 8vo.

——(*Cumberland's British Theatre*, vol. i.) London, 1829, 12mo.

——(*Penny National Library*.) London [1830], 8vo.

——(*Sinnett's Family Drama*.) Hamburg, 1834, 8vo.

——(*The Acting Drama*.) London, 1834, 8vo.

——Another edition. [With an introduction and German notes, by H. Croll.] Stuttgart, 1842, 16mo.

No. v. of " The British and American Theatre."

——(*Lacy's Acting Edition of Plays*, etc., vol. xxv.) London, [1856], 12mo.

——(*British Drama*, vol. i.) London, 1864, 8vo.

——Truchy's edition. She Stoops to Conquer. To which are added biographical and critical remarks, besides numerous notes in French, etc. Paris, 1866, 16mo.

——Another edition. London, 1883, 32mo.

——Another edition, with Drawings by Edwin A. Abbey. Decorations by Alfred Parsons. Introduction by Austin Dobson. New York, 1887, large fol.

A London edition of ths work was issued the same year.

VI. SELECTIONS.

The Beauties of the Magazines, consisting of essays by Colman, Goldsmith, etc. 2 vols. London, 1772, 12mo.

——Another edition. 2 vols. Altenburgh, 1775, 8vo.

The Beauties of Goldsmith, consisting of selections from his prose and poetry, by A. Howard. London [1834], 12mo.

Selections from the writings of O. G. Fifth edition. Calcutta, 1879, 12mo.

VII. MISCELLANEOUS.

The Art of Poetry on a new plan : illustrated with a great variety of examples from the best English poets, etc. [Attributed to O. G.] 2 vols. London, 1762, 12mo.

The Beauties of English Poesy. Selected by O. G. [and Preface written by him]. 2 vols. London, 1767, 12mo.

The British Magazine, or Monthly Repository for Gentlemen and Ladies. [Edited by T. Smollett, assisted by O. G.] 8 vols. London [1760-67], 8vo.

The Comic Romance of Monsieur Scarron, translated by O. G. 2 vols. Dublin [1780], 12mo.

A Concise History of Philosophy and Philosophers. [Translated from the French of J. H. S. Formey by O. G.] London, 1766, 12mo.

A General History of the World, from the Creation to the present time, etc. By W. Guthrie. [Preface written by O. G.] 13 vols. London, 1764-67, 8vo.

The History of Little Goody Two-Shoes; otherwise called Mrs. Margery Two-Shoes, etc. Third edition. [Attributed to O. G.] London, 1766, 16mo.

The Lilliputian Magazine; or, the Young Gentleman and Lady's Golden Library. [Edited by O. G.?]. London [1752?] 12mo.

Memoirs of a Protestant condemned to the Gallies of France for his Religion. [Translated by O. G.]. 2 vols. London, 1758, 12mo.

Plutarch's Lives abridged from the Greek, illustrated with notes and reflections, and embellished with copperplate cuts. [By O. G. and Joseph Collier.] 7 vols. London, 1762, 18mo.

Poems for Young Ladies, being a collection of the best pieces in our language. [Preface written by O. G.]. London, 1767, 12mo.

——A new edition. London, 1770, 8vo.

——Another edition. London, 1785, 12mo.

A Pretty Book of Pictures for Little Masters and Misses; or, Tommy Trip's History of Beasts and Birds. The ninth edition. [Attributed to O. G.]. London, 1767, 24mo.

——A Pretty Book of Pictures for Little Masters and Misses; or, Tommy Trip's History of Beasts and Birds. With a familiar description of each in verse and prose. To which is prefix'd the History of Little Tom Trip himself. The fifteenth edition, embellished with charming engravings on wood from the original blocks engraved by T. Bewick for T. Saint of Newcastle in 1779, etc. London, 1867, 4to.

VIII.

REVIEWS AND ESSAYS.

Reviews—
Monthly Review. — April 1757, vol. xvi., p. 377, Mythology and Poetry of the Celtes.—May 1757, vol. xvi., p. 426, Home's Tragedy of 'Douglas.'—May 1757, vol. xvi., p. 443, Thornton and Colman's Connoisseur. —May 1757, vol. xvi., p. 473, Burke on the Sublime and Beautiful. — June 1757, vol. xvi., p. 530, On Smollett's History of England. — June 1757, vol. xvi., p. 559, Charlevoix's History of Paraguay.— June 1757, Saxe's Memoirs of the Art of War.—July 1757, vol. xvii., p. 44, De Polignac's Anti-Lucretius. — July 1757, Two Novels (1) The Mother-in-Law, or the Innocent Sufferer, (2) the Fair Citizen, etc.— July 1757, vol. xvii., p. 50, Hanway's Journey; Essay on Tea, etc.—July 1757, vol. xvii., p. 81, Memoirs of Madame de Maintenon.—August 1757, vol.

xvii., p. 154, Voltaire's Universal History. — August 1757, Rabener's Satirical Letters.— August 1757, Letters from an Armenian in Ireland. — September 1757, vol. xvii., p. 228, The Epigoniad. — September 1757, vol. xvii., p. 239, Gray's Odes. — December 1758, vol. xix., p. 513, Enquiries concern- the First Inhabitants, etc., of Europe. — December 1758, vol. xix., p. 519, Bayly's Introduction to Languages. — December 1758, vol. xix., p. 523, Burton's Greek Tragedies. — December 1758, vol. xix., p. 524, Cicero's Tusculan Disputations.

Critical Review. — November 1757, vol. iv., p. 402, Mr. Massey's Translation of Ovid's Fasti.—January 1759 vol. vii., p. 26, Female Conduct. An Essay.—January 1759, vol. vii., p. 38, Barrett's Ovid's Epistles. —February 1759, vol. vii., p. 103, Spenser's Faerie Queene.— March 1759, vol. vii., p. 260, Langhorne's Death of Adonis, from the Greek of Bion.— March 1759, vol. vii., p. 270, Goquet on the Origin and Progress of Laws, Arts, and Sciences. — April 1759, vol. vii., p. 369, Ward's System of Oratory.—May 1759, vol. vii., p. 434, [Murphy's] Orphan of China.—June 1759, vol. vii., p. 483, Young's Conjectures on Original Composition. — June 1759, vol. vii., p. 486, [Formey's] Philosophical Miscellanies.—June 1759, vol. vii., p. 504, Van Egmont's Travels through Europe, Asia Minor, etc.—June 1759, vol. vii., p. 535, Montesquieu's Miscel-

laneous Pieces. — July and September 1759, vol. viii., p. 1 and 208, Butler's Remains in Verse and Prose.—July 1759- Horace modernized. — August 1759, vol. viii., p. 89, Guicciardini's History of Italy.—August 1759, vol. viii., p. 97, The Works of the Rev. William Hawkins. — August 1759, vol. viii., p. 165, [Modern Novels] Jemima and Louisa, etc. — March 1760, vol. ix., p. 235, Dunkin's Epistle to Lord Chesterfield.

Collected Essays—

Literary Magazine. — January 1757, and January, February 1758, The History of Our Own Times.—January 1758, a Poetical Scale.—Phanor; or the Butterfly Pursuit: a Political Allegory. — February 1758, Sequel to the Poetical Balance, being Miscellaneous Thoughts on English Poets.—February- May 1758, Four Letters, The History of our own Language. *Busy Body.*—October 13, 1759, A Description of Various Clubs. — October 20, 1759, On Public Rejoicings for Victory. *Public Ledger.*—January 17, 1760, Letter on Abuse of our Enemies. —January 22, 1760, The Goddess of Silence.—February 16, 1760, The Description of a Wow-Wow in the Country. *British Magazine.* — February 1760, On the Different Schools of Music. — February - April 1760, A Reverie at the Boar's Head Tavern in Eastcheap.— May 1760, p. 129, A Dream.— June 1760, p. 348, A Parallel between Mrs. Vincent and Miss

Brent. — June 1760, p. 369, The Distresses of a Common Soldier.—July 1760, p. 320, A True History for the Ladies. — July 1760, p. 421, A Dream. [A Visit to Elysium. — The Mansion of Poetry and Taste]. —July 1760, Letter. [History of Miss Stanton].—July 1760, Carolan, the last Irish Bard.— August 1760, On National Prejudices.—On the Proper Engagement of Life. — October 1760, Adventures of a Strolling Player.—December, 176), National Union. — July 1761-January 1763, i. Upon Taste; ii. On the Cultivation of Taste; iii. The Origin of Poetry; iv. On Poetry, as distinguished from other writing; v. On Metaphors; vi. On Hyperbole; vii. On Versification. — January 1762, Letter : Female Warriors: containing a humble Proposal for Augmenting the Forces of Great Britain.

Lady's Magazine.—The Progress of Politeness : Rules enjoined to be observed at a Russian Assembly. — On the English Clergy, and Popular Preachers. —April 1761, Zenim and Galhinda.

Westminster Magazine.—January 1773, The History of a Poet's Garden.—Essay on the Theatre; or, a comparison between sentimental and laughing Comedy.— February 1773, A Register of Scotch Marriages.—The History of Cyrillo Padovano, the noted Sleep-walker.

Universal Magazine.—April 1774, On Friendship.

IX. APPENDIX.

BIOGRAPHY, CRITICISM, ETC.

Annual Register. — The Annual Register. London, 1758, etc., 8vo.
   References to Goldsmith in vols. 7, 9, 12, 13, 16, 17, 20-23, 29, 33, 36-38, 40, 43, 44, 61.

Bewick, T.—[Woodcuts to Goldsmith's and Parnell's Poems, etc.]. [1795], folio.

Bingley, William.— Biographical Conversations, etc. London, 1818, 8vo.
   Oliver Goldsmith, pp. 176-187.

Biographical Magazine.—Lives of the Illustrious (*The Biographical Magazine*). London, 1852, 8vo.
   Oliver Goldsmith, vol. ii., pp. 99-120.

Black, William. — Goldsmith. (*English Men of Letters*). London 1878, 8vo.

Boswell, James.—The Life of Samuel Johnson, etc. 2 vols. London, 1791, 4to.
   Numerous references to Goldsmith.

British Plutarch. — The British Plutarch, containing the Lives of the most eminent Statesmen, etc. Third edition. 8 vols. London, 1791, 8vo.
   Life of Oliver Goldsmith, vol. viii., pp. 192-201.

Brydges, Sir S. E. — Censura Literaria, etc. 10 vols. London, 1805–9, 8vo.
   Dr. Oliver Goldsmith, vol. v., pp. 54-75.

Cary, Henry Francis.—Lives of the English Poets, from Johnson to Kirke White. London, 1846, 8vo.
   Oliver Goldsmith, pp. 222-246.

Cruikshank, George. — Illustrations of Smollett, Fielding, and Goldsmith, in a series of forty-one plates, designed and engraved by George Cruikshank. Accompanied by descriptive extracts. London, 1832, 8vo.

Cumberland, Richard.— Memoirs of Richard Cumberland, written by himself, etc. London, 1806, 4to.
Numerous references to Goldsmith.

Davies, Thomas. Memoirs of the Life of David Garrick, etc. A new edition. 2 vols. London, 1780, 8vo.
Dr. Goldsmith, vol. ii., pp. 142-164.

Dawson, George. — Biographical Lectures. London, 1886, 8vo.
Oliver Goldsmith, pp. 172-190.

De Quincey, Thomas.—De Quincey's Works. 14 vols. London, 1853-60, 8vo.
Oliver Goldsmith, vol. vi., pp. 194-233.

Encyclopædia Britannica. — The Encyclopædia Britannica. Eighth edition. Edinburgh, 1856, 4to.
Article, Goldsmith, by T. B. Macaulay, vol. x. Reprinted also in Ninth Edition.

Forster, John.—The Life and Adventures of Oliver Goldsmith. A Biography : in four books. London, 1848, 8vo.
——Second edition. 2 vols. London, 1854, 8vo.

Forsyth, William.—The Novels and Novelists of the Eighteenth Century, etc. London, 1871, 8vo.
Goldsmith, pp. 305-312.

Giles, Henry.—Lectures and Essays. 2 vols. Boston [U.S.], 1850, 8vo.
Oliver Goldsmith, vol. i., pp. 218-257.

Goldsmith, Oliver.—An Impartial Character of the late Doctor Goldsmith ; with a word to his encomiasts. A Poem. London, 1774, 4to.

Goldsmith, Oliver. The Druid's Monument, a tribute to the Memory of Doctor Oliver Goldsmith. By the Author of the "Cave of Morar." London, 1774, 4to.
——A Monody on the death of Dr. Oliver Goldsmith. London, 1774, 4to.
——De Dorppredikant ; Tooneelspel, in vyf bedryven [and in prose], founded on the "Vicar of Wakefield" (*Nieuwe* Spectatoriaale Schouwburg, deel 23). Amsterdam, 1793, 8vo.

Hamilton, Walter.—Parodies of the works of English and American authors, collected and annotated by W. H. London, 1886, 4to.
Oliver Goldsmith, vol. iii., pp. 3-20.

Hawes, William.--An account of the late Dr. Goldsmith's illness so far as relates to the Exhibition of Dr. James's Powder, etc. London, 1780, 8vo.
—— Fourth edition, with corrections and an appendix. London, 1780, 8vo.

Hirātāla, Pāla.—Annotations on Goldsmith's Vicar, containing copious explanations of difficult passages, etc. Part I. Calcutta, 1881, 12mo.

Howitt, William.—Homes and Haunts of the most eminent British Poets. Third edition. London, 1857, 8vo.
Goldsmith, pp. 195-228.

Hunt, Leigh.—Classic Tales, serious and lively, etc. London, 1806, 12mo.
Critical Essay on the Writings and Genius of Goldsmith, by Leigh Hunt, vol. i., pp. 41-80.

Hutton, Laurence. — Literary Landmarks of London. London [1885], 8vo.
Oliver Goldsmith, pp. 118-126.

Irving, Washington.—The Life of Oliver Goldsmith, with selections from his writings. 2 vols. New York, 1844, 12mo.
Numerous editions.

Jeaffreson, J. Cordy.—Novels and Novelists from Elizabeth to Victoria. 2 vols. London, 1858, 8vo.
O. Goldsmith, vol. i., pp. 223-257.

Kalisch, M. M.—The Life and Writings of Oliver Goldsmith ; two lectures delivered to a village audience. London, 1860, 8vo.

Karsten, Johannes.—Oliver Goldsmith. Ein Gesammtbild seines Lebens und seiner Werke. Strassburg, 1873, 8vo.

Kent, W. Charles.—Dreamland, with other poems. London, 1862, 8vo.
Goldsmith at Edgeware (13 verses), pp. 67-71.

Laun, Adolf.—Oliver Goldsmith. Sein Leben, sein Charakter und seine Werke. Berlin, 1876, 8vo.

Lautenhammer, Dr.—Oliver Goldsmith. A biographical sketch. Munich, 1874, 8vo.

Leslie, Charles Robert.—Life and Times of Sir J. Reynolds : with notices of some of his contemporaries. Commenced by C. R. L., and continued by T. Taylor, etc. 2 vols. London, 1865, 8vo.
Numerous references to Goldsmith.

Macaulay, Lord. — The Miscellaneous Writings, Speeches, and Poems of Lord Macaulay. London, 1880, 8vo.
Oliver Goldsmith, vol. ii., pp. 40-58.

Mangin, Rev. Edward.—An Essay on Light Reading, etc. London, 1818, 8vo.
Oliver Goldsmith, pp. 117-152, 159-176.

Mason, William Shaw. A statistical account or parochial survey of Ireland. 3 vols. Dublin, 1814-49, 8vo.
The Goldsmith Family, vol. iii., pp. 356-366.

Melmoth, Courtney, [*i.e.*, Samuel Jackson Pratt.]—The Tears of Genius. Occasioned by the death of Dr. Goldsmith. London, 1774, 4to.

Minto, William.—A Manual of English Prose Literature, etc. Third edition. Edinburgh, 1886, 8vo.
Oliver Goldsmith, pp. 461-473.

Nichols, John.—Literary Anecdotes of the eighteenth century, etc. 9 vols. London, 1812-15, 8vo.
Numerous references to Goldsmith.

——Illustrations of the Literary History of the eighteenth century, etc. 8 vols. London, 1817-58, 8vo.
Numerous references to Goldsmith.

Nicoll, Henry J.—Landmarks of English Literature. London 1883, 8vo.
O. Goldsmith, pp. 249-256.

Northcote, James. — Memoirs of Sir Joshua Reynolds, etc. London, 1813, 4to.
Numerous references to Goldsmith.

Notes and Queries.—General Index to Notes and Queries. Five series. London, 1856-1880, 4to.
Numerous references to Goldsmith.

Percy, Sholto, [*i.e.* J. C. Robertson.]
The Percy Anecdotes. 20 vols.
London, 1823, 12mo.
Numerous anecdotes of Gold-
smith.

Prior, Sir James.—The Life of
Oliver Goldsmith, from a variety
of original sources. [With
extracts from his correspondence.] 2 vols. London, 1837,
8vo.

Read, Charles A.—The Cabinet of
Irish Literature, etc. London,
1879, 8vo.
Goldsmith, with portrait, vol. i.,
pp. 264-289.

Rossetti, W. M.—Lives of Famous
Poets. London [1885], 8vo.
Oliver Goldsmith, pp. 161-175.

Ryan, Richard.—A Biographical
Dictionary of the Worthies of
Ireland, etc. 2 vols. London,
1821, 8vo.
Oliver Goldsmith, vol. ii.. pp.
181-197.

Saure, Dr., and Weischer, Dr.—
Biographies of English Poets,
etc. Leipzig, 1880, 8vo.
Oliver Goldsmith, pp. 118-142.

Spilsbury, F.—Free Thoughts on
Quacks and their medicines,
occasioned by the death of Dr.
Goldsmith and Mr. Scawen, etc.
London, 1776, 8vo.

Stanhope, P. H., *Lord Mahon.*—
History of England. London,
1851, 8vo.
Dr. Goldsmith, vol. vi , pp. 482,
483.

Taine, H. A. — Histoire de la
Littérature Anglaise. 4 Tom.
Paris, 1863-64, 8vo.
Goldsmith, tom. iii., 330-336.

——History of English Literature.
Translated by H. Van Laun.
New edition. 4 vols. Edin-
burgh, 1873-74, 8vo.
Goldsmith, vol. iii., pp. 311-316.

Taylor, Tom.—The Vicar of Wakefield ; an original drama in

three acts [and in prose by T.
Taylor. Founded upon O. G.'s
novel]. London [1851], 12mo.
Lacy's Acting Edition of Plays,
etc., vol. ii.

Thackeray, W. M.—The English
Humourists of the Eighteenth
Century. Second edition. Lon-
don, 1853, 8vo.
Sterne and Goldsmith, pp. 269-
322.

——The Works of W. M. T.
Miscellaneous Essays, etc. vol.
xxiii. London, 1886, 8vo.
Dr. Johnson and Goldsmith. This
drawing was first published in the
North British Review of February
1864, in Dr. John Brown's article on
Thackeray.

Thrale, *aft.* Piozzi, Mrs.—Auto-
biography, letters, and literary
remains. 2 vols. London,
1861, 8vo.
References to Goldsmith.

Vernon, G. E. Harcourt.—On the
life and writings of O. G. A
lecture before the members of
the Newark Mechanics' Insti-
tute, Feb. 2, 1853. London,
1854, 8vo.

Watkins, John. — Characteristic
Anecdotes of men of learning
and genius, etc. London, 1808,
8vo.
Oliver Goldsmith, pp. 513-528.

Welsh, Charles.—A Bookseller of
the Last Century, being some
account of the life of John Newbery, etc. London, 1885, 8vo.
Numerous references to Goldsmith.

Welsh, Alfred H.—Development
of English Literature and Language. 2 vols. Chicago, 1882,
8vo.
Goldsmith, vol. ii., pp. 203-221.

Whiteside, Rt. Hon. James.—
Oliver Goldsmith, his friends
and his critics ; a lecture
delivered before the Dublin
Young Men's Christian Associa-

tion, etc., Jan. 8, 1862, Dublin, 1862, 8vo.

MAGAZINE ARTICLES.

Goldsmith, Oliver. — European Magazine, vol. 24, 1793, pp. 91-95, 170-174, 258-263.— Portfolio, vol. 6, N.S., 1811, pp. 210-225.— Dublin University Magazine, vol. 7, 1836, pp. 30-54. — North American Review, by E. T. Channing, vol. 45, 1837, pp. 91-116.—Southern Literary Messenger, by H. T. Tuckerman, vol. 6, 1840, pp. 267-274. — Penny Magazine, vol. 11, 1842, pp. 25-28.—New York Review, vol. 1, p. 1, etc. —Museum of Foreign Literature, vol. 6, p. 1, etc., and vol. 31, p. 126, etc.—Edinburgh Review, by Lord Lytton, vol. 88, 1848, pp. 193-225 ; same article, Littell's Living Age, vol. 18, pp. 345-358.— North British Review, vol. 9, 1848, pp. 187-212 ; same article, Eclectic Magazine, vol. 14, pp. 365-380, and in Littell's Living Age, vol. 17, pp. 577-588.— Methodist Quarterly Review, vol. 31, 1849, pp. 351-377.— American Whig Review, vol. 10, 1849, pp. 498-512.—Blackwood's Edinburgh Magazine, vol. 67, 1850, pp. 137-152, 297-308 ; same article, Eclectic Magazine, vol. 20, pp. 87-100 and 184-195. — Illustrated Exhibitor, vol. 2, 1852, pp. 184-187. —Harper's New Monthly Magazine, by T. B. Macaulay, vol. 14, 1857, pp. 633-639 (from the Encyclopædia Britannica).—Art Journal (Illustrated), 1864, pp.

Goldsmith, Oliver.
305-307 and 326, 327.—Sharpe's London Magazine, by E. Townbridge, vol. 33, N.S., 1868, pp. 260-265.—Appleton's Journal of Literature, by G. M. Towle, vol 11, 1874, pp. 459-462.— Harper's New Monthly Magazine (Illustrated), by G. M. Towle, vol. 48, 1874, pp. 681-692.

——*Adventures of.* Chambers's Edinburgh Journal, vol. 9, N.S., 1848, pp. 343-347.

——*and Dr. Johnson.* De Bow's Review, vol. 28, 1860, pp. 504-513.

——*and his biographers.* Dublin University Magazine, vol. 32, 1848, pp. 315-337 ; same article, Littell's Living Age, vol. 19, pp. 145-161.—Sharpe's London Journal, by Frederick Lawrence, vol. 11. pp. 1-10 ; same article, Littell's Living Age, vol. 24, 1850, pp. 337-346.

——*and La Bruyère.* Argosy, by W. Clark Russell, vol. 5, 1868, pp. 263-269.

——*Anecdotes of.* Annual Register, vol. 17, 1774, pp. 29-34.

——*Centenary of.* Dublin University Magazine, by W. J. Fitzpatrick, vol. 83, 1874, pp. 438-446.

——*Country of.* Eclectic Review vol. 2, N.S., 1859, pp. 597-618.

——*Deserted Village.* Monthly Review, vol. 42, 1770, pp. 440-445.—Portfolio, by C. R., vol. 4, 3rd series, 1814, pp. 315-321. —Belgravia, by J. O'Byrne Croke, vol. 10, 3rd Series, pp. 98-102.

—— ——*Deserted Village Illustrated by Etching Club.* Black-

Goldsmith, Oliver.
  wood's Edinburgh Magazine,
  vol. 51, 1842, pp. 122-129.
—— ——*Visit to Deserted Village.*
  Monthly Religious Magazine,
  vol. 27, p. 221, etc.
——*Early Haunts of.* Irish
  Monthly Magazine, by J. J.
  Kelly, vol. 7, 1879, pp. 194-205.
——*Enquiry into the present state
  of Polite Learning in Europe.*
  Monthly Review, vol. 21, 1759,
  pp. 381-389.
——*Forster's Life of.* New Monthly
  Magazine, vol. 83, 1848, pp. 98-
  103.—British Quarterly Review,
  vol. 8, 1848, pp. 1-25.—Quarterly Review, vol. 95, 1854, pp.
  394-448; same article, Littell's
  Living Age, vol. 7, 2nd Series,
  pp. 531-558, and Eclectic Magazine, vol. 34, pp. 1-31.
—— *Fortune and Friends of.*
  National Magazine, vol. 9, p.
  209, etc., and 416, etc.
——*Gossip about.* Bentley's Mis-
  cellany, vol. 24, 1848, pp. 193-
  198.
——*Grave of.* New Monthly
  Magazine, vol. 124, 1862, pp.
  426-430.
——*History of England.* Monthly
  Review, vol. 45, 1771, pp. 436-
  444.
——*in the Temple.* London Magazine, by T. H. Gibson, vol. 3,
  1877, pp. 97-100.
——*Irving's Life of.* North American Review, by C. M. Kirkland,
  vol. 70, 1850, pp. 265-289.—
  Christian Observer, vol. 51, 1851,
  pp. 469-486.
——*Life of.* Portfolio, vol. 13,
  4th Series, 1822, pp. 473-487.
  —London Magazine, vol. 5,
  1822, pp. 105-112.
——*Macaulay on.* Dublin Review, vol. 43, 1857, pp. 82-107.

Goldsmith, Oliver.
——*Miscellaneous Works of.* British Critic, vol. 20, 1802, pp.
  295-298.—Monthly Review, vol.
  38, 1802, pp. 44-53.
——*Natural History.* Monthly
  Review, vol. 52, 1775, pp. 310-
  314.
——*Personality of.* Dublin University Magazine, by R. B. S.
  Knowles, vol. 88, 1876, pp. 352-
  367.
——*Poetry of.* Art Journal, illustrated, vol. 3, N.S., 1851, p.
  120.
——*Prior's Life of.* Quarterly
  Review, vol. 57, 1836, pp. 273-
  324. — Edinburgh Review, by
  W. Empson, vol. 65, 1837,
  pp. 204-244.—Fraser's Magazine,
  vol. 15, 1837, pp. 387-400.-
  Tait's Edinburgh Magazine, vol.
  4, N.S., 1837, pp. 238-258, and
  vol. 5, pp. 163, 164. — Eclectic
  Review, vol. 1, N.S., 1837, pp.
  114-131; vol. 2, N.S., 1837,
  pp. 27-41.—American Quarterly
  Review, vol. 21, 1837, pp. 460-
  515.—North American Review,
  by E. T. Channing, vol. 45,
  1837, pp. 91-116. — Monthly
  Review, vol. 1, N.S., pp. 163-
  170.—New Monthly Magazine,
  vol. 49, 1837, pp. 282-286.
——*Roman History.* Monthly
  Review, vol. 41, 1769, pp. 183-
  190.
—— *She Stoops to Conquer.*
  Monthly Review, vol. 48, 1773,
  pp. 309-314.
——*Traveller.* Monthly Review,
  vol. 32, 1765, pp. 47-55.
——*Vicar of Wakefield.* Blackwood's Edinburgh Magazine,
  vol. 53, 1843, pp. 771-779.—
  Athenæum, Dec. 1885, pp. 835-
  837.

X. CHRONOLOGICAL LIST OF WORKS.